The Horse and Pony Care Handbook

The Horse and Pony Care Handbook

Amanda Lang

ISLAND BOOKS

This edition published in 2003 by
S. WEBB & Son (Distributors) LTD
Telford Place, Pentraeth Road,
Menai Bridge,
Isle of Anglesey, LL59 5RW

D&S Books Ltd
Kerswell,
Parkham Ash, Bideford
Devon, England
EX39 5PR

e-mail us at:-
enquiries@dsbooks.fsnet.co.uk

This edition printed 2003

ISBN 1-856057-59-3

Creative Director: Sarah King
Editor: Anna Southgate
Project editor: Judith Millidge
Photographer: Paul Forrester
Designer: Axis Design Editions

Printed in Singapore

This book was set in Futura BT, Akzidenz Grotesk & GillSans

1 3 5 7 9 10 8 6 4 2

Contents

Introduction

Having a pony of your own can be one of the best things about growing up. As a child I spent most of my time begging and pleading with my parents to buy me one. Of course, I was only six or seven years old at the time and had no idea how much of a responsibility caring for an animal actually was. Neither did I think about the costs – all I wanted was to gallop carefree along the beach on my own pony. So I continued to plead with my parents for years – at least twenty times a day and at every birthday and Christmas. Finally, one winter, when I was in my early teens, I got a pony on winter loan from the local riding school. He was short, fat and hairy, and I was sure we would take on the world together!

I spent most of my waking hours with my pony, and would have slept in the stable if I had been allowed to. While my teenage friends were experimenting with make-up and window-shopping for clothes, I would be out in my wellies and stinking of horses. Sadly, spring came round all too quickly and I was heartbroken when my pony had to be returned to the stables to work for the summer.

From that time on I worked at the stables at weekends and during school holidays in exchange for rides. When I left school I went on to study at an equestrian centre, where I became a working pupil. After two years I gained my qualifications as a riding instructor. Since then I have taught many children to ride and have owned and ridden many different horses and ponies. I believe a true love of horses stays with you for life, and the sight of them grazing quietly on a summer's day always fills me with immense pleasure.

I now live on a farm and have four daughters and, needless to say, a selection of ponies that I could only have dreamt of as a child. With this book, I would like to show you how to care for your pony properly so that you have a long and happy time together. If you are still waiting for that day to come, then at least when it does you will be well prepared.

Horse and Pony Basics

Horse and Pony Basics

There are many breeds of horses and ponies, ranging from very small ponies just a few feet high, to large cart and heavy horses weighing over a ton. Horses are also categorized into types, as well as breeds, such as hunter or hack, for example.

THOROUGHBRED.

Horse breeds

The characteristics of modern horse breeds have largely developed according to where in the world they originated. Some breeds show the influence of their Oriental forebears, for example, while others can trace their origins to European stock.

There are three main types of horse - heavy (also known as Cold bloods), Light (also known as Warm bloods) and ponies. Cross breeding between the types makes some differences less distinct, but in general all horses fall wihin one of these types. In some cases there is a conflict of opinion as to whether a certain breed should be classified as a pony or a horse, but a pony is generally stockier than a horse, and less than 15 hands high.

Breed classificaton is quite strict, and in order to classify as belonging to a particular breed, a horse needs to conform with certain key standards. Breed conformation largely depends on the purpose of the horse. The most important aspect being the physical proportions. These must be well-balanced in order for the horse to perform at its optimum level. Certain breeds also restrict colour variations.

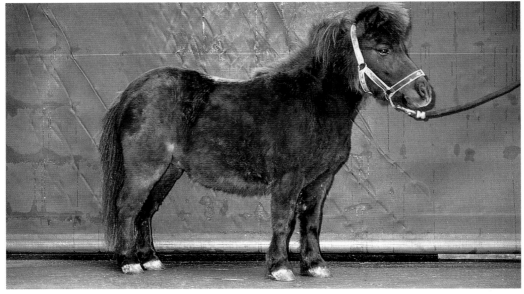

SHETLAND PONY.

The Thoroughbred horse (see previous page) is one of the most popular and easily recogniseable breeds, thanks largely to its role as a racehorse, and modern horses can trace their lineage back to three sires - *The Darley Arabian, The Godolphin Arabian* and *The Byerley Turk*.Throughbred colours are generally brown or chestnut, with height ranging between 14-17 hands.

The Shetland pony is one of the most well-known and loved of the pony breeds. It is hardy, sturdy and generally even-tempered, and often found as a mount for young children.

The Norwegian Fjord is another stocky pony, suitable for light draft work.

The Russian Don is best known as being a cavalry warhorse, and its stamina and endurance make it eminently suitable as a long distance riding horse today. it's height is usually between 15-16.5 hands, with bay and chestnut being standard colours.

Used primarily in showjumping and other performance sports, the Dutch warmblood is generally 15-16 hands high, with any solid colour being allowed.

NORWEGIAN FJORD.

BRITISH WARMBLOOD.

DON.

DUTCH WARMBLOOD.

Colours

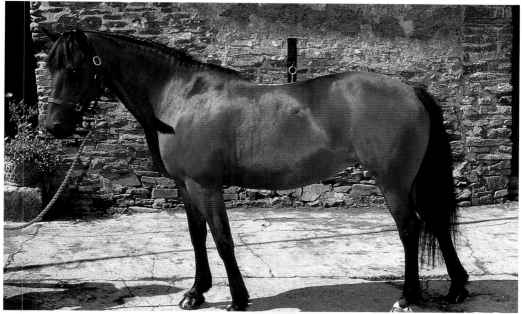

AN EXAMPLE OF BAY COLOURING.

Horses and ponies vary in colour from one season to another. Some breeds also change colour as they get older.

Black

Black horses and ponies are usually jet black all over, sometimes with a few white markings.

Brown

Brown horses and ponies can be dark brown, (almost black) or brown. They have dark brown manes, tails and legs.

Bay

Bay colouring varies from light, reddish brown to dark brown. Bay horses and ponies have black manes and tails and are black below the knee or hock. Sometimes they also have some white markings.

Chestnut

This is a ginger, reddish/orange colour and could be darker, more chestnut colour. The mane is a similar colour to the body. The lighter chestnuts sometimes have a cream-coloured mane and tail. This is known as a 'flaxen' mane and tail.

Grey

Greys have black skin with white and black hairs. They vary from very light to dark iron-grey in colour and may have dappled areas. A flea-bitten grey is when the black hairs appear in tufts through the coat.

Palomino

Palomino horses and ponies are golden-yellow with a flaxen mane and tail.

Piebald

Piebald horses and ponies are black with large, irregular white patches.

A FINE GREY.

SKEWBALD.

Skewbald

Skewbald horses and ponies are any other colour with large patches of white.

Dun

Dun horses and ponies are a mousy colour, often with a black stripe along the spine and a black mane and tail.

Roan

This is when the coat is mixed with white hairs. For example, a bay pony may have a lot of white hairs in its coat, giving it a red tinge. It could also have white markings. Chestnut or strawberry roan is when the coat is predominantly chestnut with white hairs mixed in it resulting in a strawberry colour. A blue roan is a predominantly black or very dark brown coat with white hairs mixed in, giving it a blue tinge. Blue roans usually have black legs below the knee and hock.

Markings

Some horses and ponies have markings of white hair. Such markings are evident from birth rather than those that might grow following damage to the skin.

STRIPE AND SNIP.

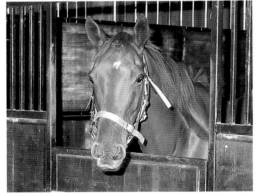

STAR.

Star

A patch of white hair found on a pony's forehead and which varies in shape and size.

Stripe

A slim strip of white down a pony's face.

Blaze

A white forehead and a white strip down the face, which is wider than the nasal bone.

Snip

This is a small patch of white hair found between the nostrils.

Hair whorls

These are usually found on either side of the neck, on the crest or on the forehead. They are small patches where hair grows in a different direction to that of the rest of the coat.

WHITE MARKINGS ON THE LEGS.

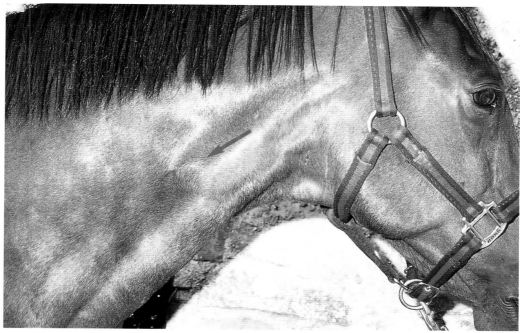

HAIR WHORL.

Wall eye

This is when a horse's or pony's eye looks very different, usually pale and blue. It is caused by a lack of pigment in the iris and often only affects one eye.

White markings on the legs

This is described according to how far the white reaches up the leg. For example, white pastern, white coronet or white fetlock. White that extends above the fetlock and up the cannon bone is sometimes called a 'sock', and white that reaches just below the knee is sometimes called a 'stocking'.

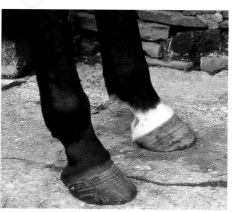

WHITE MARKINGS.

Measuring

ALWAYS MEASURE A HORSE'S HEIGHT ON LEVEL GROUND.

Horses and ponies are measured in hands. One hand is 4 inches, so a horse that is 13½ hands would be described as 13.2 h. Another 2 inches and it would be described as 14.0 h. Ponies over 14.2 h high are often referred to as horses, although it is not just a matter of height – type needs to be taken into account as well. Shetland ponies are almost always measured in inches and so are described as 38 in., for example. Horses and ponies should be measured on level ground using a marked stick. Height is measured from the ground up to the highest point of the withers.

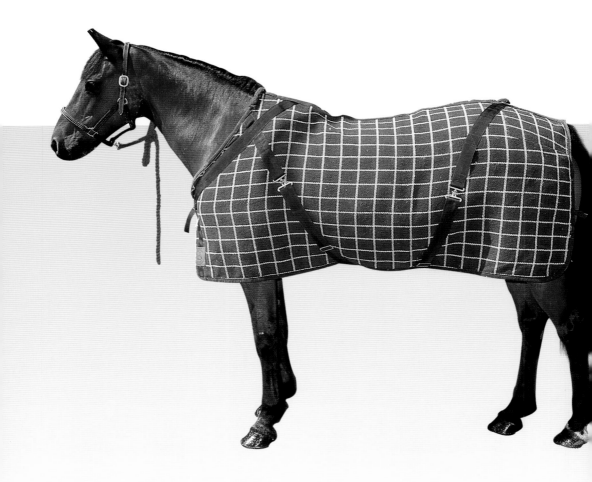

Care and Management

Keeping a pony at livery

In an ideal world all pony-mad children would have a stable and paddock at the bottom of their garden. If you don't have the facilities to keep a pony at home, however, you could consider the possibility of keeping one at a livery yard. Make sure you choose your livery yard or riding school carefully, as standards may vary. Take a knowledgeable friend along with you to visit prospective yards – they may spot things that you miss. A yard should be clean, well-maintained, and the ponies should be in good condition. Some riding schools run a working livery, with little or no money involved, where they use your pony to give lessons while you are not using him. This system can work well as long as you don't mind sharing your pony.

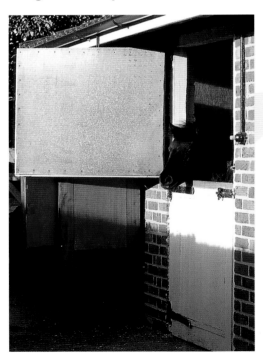

Grass livery is probably the cheapest way to keep a pony if you have a hardy one that can live out all year round. You will still need to visit your pony twice a day, but if you are busy with school or work this method may suit you well. Native British ponies, such as Dartmoor and Exmoor ponies, are especially suited to a grass livery and are used to outdoor conditions.

THERE ARE MANY ADVANTAGES TO STABLES.

HARDY PONIES CAN LIVE OUTSIDE ALL YEAR.

HORSES ARE HERD ANIMALS AND NEED COMPANY.

Full livery is when the pony is cared for completely, including feeding, mucking out, exercising and his general well being. This is a good option if you are very busy, but it can be expensive. You would also lose the fun and satisfaction of caring for your own pony. Do-it-yourself livery is another option where you care for the pony yourself, simply renting a field and /or a stable. This is a good option if you live nearby so that you can visit your pony twice a day. One advantage of this system is that your pony will probably have others for company. In some cases the livery yard owner may take on some of the responsibilities, such as feeding

and turning out the pony in the morning to save you one visit a day.

Before taking your pony to his new home make sure you have a proper written agreement stating the terms and conditions you have agreed to. It is a good idea to make sure that you are insured just in case your pony kicks another pony or escapes onto the road and causes an accident. Keeping your pony at a livery yard can be fun, and you may be lucky enough to find new friends to ride with, as well a knowledgeable person to consult if you have any problems.

Keeping a pony stabled

STABLES OFFER PROTECTION AND SECURITY.

veterinary treatment in a safe, confined space. You can keep a stabled pony a lot cleaner, saving time when you want to ride him and helping to keep his skin healthy. You can clip him, which will keep him even drier and more comfortable when doing a lot of work. However, bear in mind that this means you will need rugs, which can be expensive, and looking after a clipped pony is more time-consuming, as rugs need to be changed, cleaned and repaired. Stabling a pony part-time is very useful in the management of certain conditions and particularly to restrict the grazing of an overweight pony.

Ponies can become stressed when confined in a stable, especially without company, and yet there are some advantages that cannot be overlooked. The first is that you always know where your pony is. With a stabled pony, it is obviously easier to monitor how warm he is, how much feed and hay he has eaten and how much water he has drunk. When you are mucking out you will easily notice any changes in the amount of dropping or urine, which could be an indication that the pony is not feeling well. It is also easier to get a pony fit when you can accurately monitor his feed and exercise. It is much easier to administer

The disadvantages are that a pony can develop compulsive habits such as crib-biting, wind sucking and weaving, which may be copied by others in the yard. It is generally more expensive to keep a pony stabled, as you will have to provide a lot more feed, hay, rugs and bedding than for a grass-kept pony. It is also more time consuming. You must be sure to provide a stabled pony with plenty of interesting exercise, a thick comfortable bed, fresh clean water, a balanced diet, regular grooming and, as often as possible, the opportunity to be turned out with others to graze, roll and be free for a while.

Suitable stables

Your stable could be a modern purpose-built building or a converted barn. Both types have many potential dangers, and there are several aspects to consider in order ensure that your pony is safe. Firstly, it should be built on well-drained soil and facing away from the prevailing wind. It should be large, well ventilated, safe inside and strong enough to withstand a few kicks or the weight of the pony bumping against it.

The best form of stabling is a loose box. The box should be a minimum of 250–360 cm sq

THESE BOXES LOOK SPACIOUS AND LIGHT WITH PLENTY OF VENTILATION.

(10–12 ft sq) for a pony and 360 cm sq (12 ft–14 sq) for a horse. The animal should be able to move around freely and to lie down without getting 'cast' (stuck on his back). Other measures you can take to prevent him getting cast are to bank up the bedding around the walls on three sides of the box. The banks must be quite large in order to work. You can fix a 5 x 2 cm (2 x 1 in.) baton around the wall about 90 cm (three ft) from the floor all the way around the stable, which will help a horse to turn himself over.

Windows should be well maintained with any glass covered with a wire mesh to prevent the pony breaking the glass and cutting himself. A clear, non-breakable material would be preferable. Doors must be a minimum of 120 cm (4 ft) wide and should open outwards. Make sure that all the locks and bolts are in good working order. A kick bolt on the outside of the door at ground level is a good idea, where it will be out of reach for a pony. Some doors have a metal strip intended to stop the pony chewing the door. They need to be checked for any sharp edges that may cause harm. Full-height doors should be divided in two so that the top door can be hooked back for ventilation, allowing the horse to look out while

the lower part remains secure. Some stables have a grille across the top half which is useful if a pony is likely to bite or weave. It will also prevent foals from trying to jump out. Fresh air is important for keeping your pony healthy. In most circumstances, it is best to leave the top door open.

Floors are usually concrete, which is cheap and easy to install, and should have a rough or grooved surface, to prevent it becoming slippery

MESH ON A WINDOW HELPS PREVENT INJURY IF THE GLASS BREAKS.

A DIVIDED DOOR ALLOWS A HORSE TO LOOK OUT.

and dangerous. Rubber mats are quite expensive, but are ideal for putting over concrete as an extra precaution. They may save on bedding bills and, in the long run, on vet bills as well. A floor should slope slightly towards a drain either outside the stable or in the corner, and any drainage channels should be shallow and open.

Electricity makes everything a little more comfortable and is useful for clipping and lighting on winter evenings, but make sure all fittings are out of a pony's reach, preferably outside the stable with waterproof switches. Always get an electrician to check wiring and switches when using a new or different stable. Fire extinguishers should be in obvious positions and everyone in the yard should be familiar with the fire drill and the whereabouts of the nearest phone. Extinguishers must be serviced regularly.

Fit a couple of small metal rings to the wall, one to tie the pony up while you groom him, and one for the hay net. The first should be at about the height of the pony's head and should have a small loop of breakable string attached to it. Always tie the pony to the string in case he pulls back suddenly. He will break the string instead of hurting himself or you. The ring for the hay net should be higher up.

AN AUTOMATIC WATER CONTAINER.

HANG HAYNETS AT THE CORRECT HEIGHT.

Water can be easily supplied by an automatic drinking bowl which must be cleaned and checked daily. Buckets must have handles removed (to prevent the pony getting his leg stuck) and all water containers must be safe. Use rubber type containers rather than ceramic sinks or old tin containers for feed. Hay nets can be a hazard and it is worth remembering when hanging them up that they hang much lower when empty, making it easy for ponies to get their legs trapped. It is best to tie them high enough up the wall, so that they hang a good 1 m (3 ft) from the floor when empty.

If feeding a horse any concentrates, use a rubber bowl or trough at floor level. This is more natural for the animal and the rubber bowl is safe and easy to clean. However, a manger should be at chest height and in the

THESE PONIES CAN EASILY SEE THEIR STABLE MATES.

corner or on a wall. A fixed manger can be hard to clean and the pony could get stuck beneath it when rolling. Removable mangers, which you hook over a door, are more convenient and easier to keep clean.

Stalls have the advantage of offering more accommodation in less space. However, the pony is usually tied up facing a wall and can become bored easily. He will have less fresh air and may be bullied by the pony next door. Some stalls can be divided by a solid partition from the floor at least 180 cm (6 ft) high. These must be fitted correctly. Dividing walls and partitions can be dangerous if made of a flimsy material such as plywood. Some thin woods will

THIS HAYNET IS TOO LOW.

splinter if the pony kicks at them or rolls against them. Always use a strong solid material and make sure it reaches right to the floor – legs can become trapped in any gaps. If wooden bars are used, animals may kick at each other or become entangled when rolling. Stalls partitioned with a swing beam should be hung on ropes with a quick release knot, not wire. The beam should be slightly higher at the front end and should be the length of the stall.

Stable equipment

Stable equipment should be kept in good condition, particularly as some items are expensive. Quality is important, so always buy the best you can afford. Take care of it and it should give you years of use. The range of equipment – rugs, feeding items, protective clothing, bits, saddles and so on – is vast, but there are a few basic items you will need to start with. All the fashionable accessories can come later!

A NEW ZEALAND RUG PROTECTS A HORSE FROM THE COLD AND WET.

Rugs

A stabled pony will need more rugs than a grass-kept one, the latter needing a New Zealand rug or no rugs at all depending on the conditions he lives in through the winter. A stabled pony will need a stable rug, a New Zealand rug for going out in the field and a sweat rug at least. A roller is always useful for securing a blanket under the stable rug during a cool spell in winter. Exercise blankets are useful for stabled horses that have been clipped and will keep them warm while they are doing quiet work. Waterproof exercise sheets are very useful if you are going for a ride and it is likely to rain, as they keep the back and quarters dry so that, on your return, you can put your New Zealand rug or stable rug straight back on without having to dry the pony off first.

New Zealand rugs

These rugs are for outside use and are not intended to be worn in the stables. They are made of tough, waterproof fabric – usually nylon or another manmade material – although they used to be made from canvas. Nylon ones tend to be lighter for a pony to wear and dry a lot quicker following a downpour. A rug must fit properly or it will slip and move about when the pony gallops or bucks. Some rugs have a dart in the shoulder, which allows the pony to move more freely, and there are various different straps for holding it in place. A poorly fitting rug will rub and be uncomfortable. Some New Zealand rugs have attachable neck covers and hoods. They protect a horse's newly clipped head and neck from wind, cold and rain. Some rugs also have a flap to cover the top of the tail. New Zealand rugs are available in many forms so ask your saddler to help you choose one that fits well and suits your pony's lifestyle.

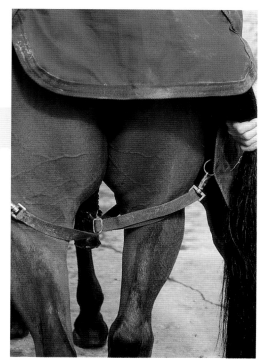

NEW ZEALAND RUGS MUST FIT PROPERLY.

STABLE RUGS PROTECT PONIES AND HORSES FROM DRAUGHTS AND CHILLS IN STABLES.

Sizes usually increase by 5 cm (3 in) at a time. To get an idea of your pony's size, measure from the centre of his chest, along his side and to the point of the buttock. A rug should cover his bottom and be deep enough to cover the belly easily and should fit snugly around the shoulders and chest. New Zealand rugs need to be kept clean and some of them can be washed. Those made of canvas need to be waterproofed every year. A spare New Zealand rug is very handy if one gets torn or very wet.

Stable rugs

Use these to keep a pony warm in the stables. They are usually made from manmade fibres and are often quilted. They vary from quite thin to very thick, so select one according to the time of year and whether your pony is clipped. For example, during early spring and autumn you will probably not need a very thick one. Another, thinner rug can be added underneath for extra warmth. As with the New Zealand rug make sure it fits correctly – it is best to ask for advice when buying your first few rugs.

THIS LIGHT THERMAL STABLE RUG IS USEFUL AS A COOLING RUG, OR AS A LIGHT RUG FOR TRAVELLING.

Spending a little more on a rug usually gets you better quality and can make a difference to the fit. Many styles and colours are available, but a good fit is of greatest importance.

Summer sheets

These are light cotton or cotton mix rugs, and are used in the summer to keep a horse free from dust and flies. They are most often used for a stabled pony.

Sweat rugs

These are light rugs that can be thrown over a horse if he has been sweating or after a bath. The rug will trap a layer of warm air but also offers ventilation and allows a horse's coat to dry off without him getting cold. Cooler rugs are also available for when a pony is sweating and needs to cool down. They are made of a different material and can act as a summer sheet, be worn under a stable rug, or as a light rug to travel in. These rugs are extremely useful and dry very quickly when washed.

Blankets

These can be used under a stable rug during a colder spell in winter, and are made either of a wool mix or of manmade fibres. To put the blanket on under a rug, place it over the pony right up to his ears and fold the two front corners at the withers, making a point at the poll. Put the stable rug on top of the blanket, positioning it a bit further forward than it needs to be. Then fold back the point of the blanket and secure everything with a roller or surcingle. Don't tighten a roller too much, or the pony will be uncomfortable, and make sure it's not twisted anywhere. Ideally, you should use a roller that has a pad on either side the spine.

Putting on and taking off a rug

Putting on a rug needs to be done quietly and correctly. It can be a very frightening experience for a pony the first few times, so get an expert to help you get him accustomed to it. Once the pony is used to the process it is very straightforward.

1 Fold the rug in half with the outside of the rug folded inside and place over the pony's withers.

4 Place the rug over the quarters.

2 Quietly do up the front strap.

3 Ñow unfold the rug.

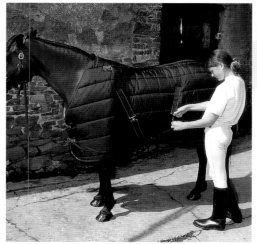

5 Do up any straps under the belly and any at the back.

6 Pull the rug backwards into place. Never pull it forwards against the lie of the hair. Be careful not to stand where you could get kicked.

1 Removing a rug correctly is just as important as putting it on properly. Work from the back forwards.

2 Make sure all straps are undone.

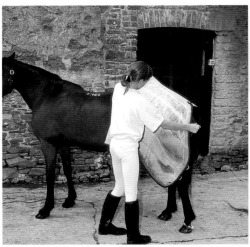

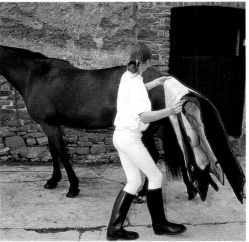

3 Fold the rug in half towards the tail.

4 Then slide it off backwards, following the way the hair lies.

Bedding

Bedding must be provided in a stable to keep your pony warm and comfortable and to protect him from injuries when rolling or lying down. It also provides cushioning for the legs and feet when standing for long periods. Whatever bedding you choose, buy the best quality available and plenty of it. Banks around the edge of a stable will help prevent your pony getting cast. A bed should be deep enough so that a pony will not touch the ground when he rolls. It must be cleaned out daily and fresh bedding added. There are several types of bedding available.

STRAW IS USUALLY READILY AVAILABLE AND REASONABLY PRICED.

Straw

The most commonly used and cheapest bedding is straw; wheat straw, easily available locally from merchants and farmers, is the best of them all as it makes a good, warm and comfortable bed. It is baled, which makes it easier to handle and to store, and needs to be kept indoors. It also rots down well and is therefore easy to dispose of.

A deep straw bed that is well banked up around the edges is attractive and inviting to a pony and drains adequately well when mucked out regularly. Barley straw makes an adequate bed, but can be prickly and irritate the skin. Oat straw tends to get wet and sodden quickly and will be readily eaten by most ponies. This is a disadvantage if you are trying to manage your pony's weight.

Be cautious when using straw, as it can be dusty and will contain mould and fungus spores that can irritate a pony's lungs. It can cause coughing and a thick discharge from the nostrils. If this does happen, the pony should not be bedded on straw or eat dry hay. This condition affects a large number of ponies, and there are other types of bedding available.

Shavings

These are more expensive than straw, but still quite economical. Only the wet patches and droppings need to be removed daily, so once you have provided a good bed it does not take a lot of shavings to keep it topped up. Shavings make a comfortable, attractive and clean looking bed. They are also free from the spores that cause some ponies problems. Wood shavings come in plastic wrapped bales and, as long as the plastic is not damaged, they can be stored outside or bought as and when you need them. The bales are heavy, however, and are therefore hard to handle. Disposing of shavings is not as easy as straw as they take a long time to rot down.

1 Remove droppings and wet patches from the straw.

2 Add fresh bedding as required.

3 Ensure the bed is deep enough and banked up around the sides.

Shredded paper

This also comes in plastic wrapped bales and can be stored outside if space is short or bought as and when needed. Paper makes a warm and comfortable bed and is cheaper than shavings but more expensive than straw. It also rots better than shavings. It is dust-free, but does tend to blow around the yard if you are not careful when mucking out.

Peat moss

This is useful where there may be a risk of fire. Wet patches must be removed daily and the bed raked. When you first put peat down it can be dusty, though this will soon settle. When rotted it is good for gardens.

Rubber mats

These can be fitted to cover the whole of the floor. Additional bedding is still advisable, but generally you need to use a lot less of it. Rubber mats are expensive to buy but are economical in the long run. They are effective in cushioning the limbs against the ground, but do not always have the appeal of a deep, warm bed.

Mucking out

HAVE YOUR EQUIPMENT READY FOR MUCKING OUT.

MUCKING OUT IS A DAILY ROUTINE.

To most pony owners, mucking out is a chore. But, with practice, the amount of time it takes can be reduced to just a few minutes. Mucking out has to be done every day and is essential in maintaining your pony's health. Like you, he will appreciate a warm, clean and comfortable bed. The equipment you will need should include a wheelbarrow, a stable fork, a shovel and a brush for sweeping. Keep the muck heap away from the stables as it will attract flies. Start a new heap every few months, leaving the first one to rot down. Keep all of your equipment tidy, and never leave equipment in the stable with a pony.

THE MUCK HEAP WILL ATTRACT FLIES, SO KEEP IT WELL AWAY FROM THE STABLES.

Mucking out a straw bed

Tie the pony up safely, preferably outside the stable or, if possible, turn him out. Put your water buckets outside. Note that this is a good time to clean the water buckets with a soft brush and to check if the water bowls of the manger needed cleaning out as well. Wheel your wheelbarrow into the stable.

1 Start with the fork, and put any droppings in the wheelbarrow. Separate the wet and dirty straw from the clean, and put the soiled straw in the wheelbarrow. Empty the wheelbarrow onto the muck heap.

2 Bank the good straw against the wall and sweep the floor, making sure you get into all the corners. Allow it to dry for a while.

3 When you are ready to spread the straw back over the floor, leave some banked up against three sides of the stable, and add fresh straw as required. The bed should be quite thick, at least the depth of the prongs of the fork.

4 Every two or three weeks you will need to wash and disinfect the floor, leaving it to dry thoroughly before replacing the straw. It is a good idea to bank the straw in a different place each time to ensure that you clean the area underneath the pile.

43

Mucking out shavings or paper

If you notice a pony has eaten a lot of his bedding, use a less palatable material. Shavings and paper are more economical if managed slightly differently and, in the short term mucking out takes up less time so may suit you better. Tie up the pony and put the water buckets outside. Use an old washing basket or something similar and a pair of rubber gloves to collect the droppings. Take out any obvious wet patches and sprinkle fresh shavings or paper over the top, banking up around the edges.

Once a week you will need to pull the whole bed up, clean the wet out and disinfect the floor. Allow the ground to dry thoroughly before replacing the bedding and topping it up with fresh shavings or paper. Peat moss can also be mucked out this way.

The deep litter method

Some people prefer this method because is saves on both time and bedding, but it does have disadvantages. When deep littering you just pick up the droppings and place fresh bedding on top of old. Then, every few weeks or months, you remove the whole bed. This method works well with shavings because they

CLEAN THE WATER CONTAINER THOROUGHLY.

FINISH BY SWEEPING THE OLD STRAW OUT.

are very absorbent and the bed does not tend to smell very much. With straw, however, if you are not careful everything can end up getting very soggy and smelly. If you chose this method, make sure that the stable is well ventilated and that the top layer of the bed is always dry, otherwise foot problems such as thrush can develop (see page 173).

Keeping a pony at grass

The amount of space needed for each pony varies depending on the quality of the grazing. As a guide, allow a minimum of between one and a half and two acres (4,000-6,000 sq m /5,000-7,500 sq yd) per pony. Some form of shelter needs to be available, which could be in the form of a thick hedge, trees, walls or a purpose-built open-fronted field shelter. A shelter tends to be used more in the summer than it does in the winter, when a pony will want to get away from the flies. Do not remove any cobwebs as these are useful for trapping flies in summer. Note that shelters with corrugated-iron roofs can get very hot in summer.

Fresh water is vital and can be provided by various means. A freshwater stream should be running constantly and pollution-free. It should not have a sandy bottom as a pony could swallow enough sand to give himself colic.

A FIELD CONTAINING BROKEN EQUIPMENT OR RUBBISH IS DANGEROUS AND UNSUITABLE FOR A PONY.

Stagnant ponds are not a suitable water supply and must be fenced off. A self-filling trough is ideal if checked often for any faults. If you have to carry water to the field then make sure it is in a suitable container with no sharp edges. Belfast sinks can get broken and may result in nasty lacerations to the lower limbs. Some ponies are incredibly accident prone so watch out for other dangerous objects. Remember that water may freeze in the winter and ponies will be unable to break even thin ice.

HORSES NEED PLENTY OF FREE TIME.

There are many advantages to keeping ponies at grass. They are natural foragers, so roaming freely to graze as they please is likely to make them much happier than being shut in a stable all day without any company and with nothing to occupy them. A pony at grass will be able to exercise himself to maintain his health. He is less likely to suffer injuries when working, and, he is also less likely to be over-enthusiastic when ridden than a pony that has been shut in stable all day.

A pony at grass generally costs less to feed because, if the grazing is good quality, then little extra feed is required during the summer months unless the pony is doing a lot of work. You should be aware, however, that too much

lush grass can be very bad for ponies, especially the native and more hardy breeds. They can develop a painful condition of the feet called laminitis (see page 168–169). During the winter months a grass-kept pony will need hay and feed according to the amount of work you require him to do. If you are only doing light hacking at weekends, for example, then hay may be all the additional feed a native pony needs. When feeding hay to several ponies out in the field, place the hay in piles in a circle, with the piles a good distance from each other so that the ponies cannot kick each other. Hay should always be good quality, and as dust free as possible.

Keeping your pony at grass all or most of the year can save a lot of time if you are busy with work or school. However, you will still need to see your pony twice a day to check for general well being, wounds and the condition of his feet. If you only visit once a day and your pony becomes ill or injures himself, is stolen or escapes from the field, it could be a long time until your next visit.

Grooming should not be overdone if a pony is living out all year as this will remove dirt and grease from his coat, which could otherwise

TRY TO KEEP YOUR PONY WITH OTHER HORSES, AS SINGLE ANIMALS BECOME LONELY.

help to keep him warm during the colder months. All you should need to do before going for a ride is to remove mud on his legs and body with a dandy brush and to brush out the mane and tail with a body brush. Do not forget to pick out and check his feet too. After a ride always brush off any sweat marks and mud before you turn him back out into the field, although he will probably go straight down and roll. Rolling is a good way for a pony to rub those parts of him that have had the saddle and bridle on, and which may cause itching. Rolling in the winter coats a pony with mud, which helps to keep him warm. Rolling in spring helps to rub out the old winter coat. It appears to be relaxing and fun and so should not be discouraged.

Stabling your pony for part of the time can be useful if you want to restrict grazing, for example, in the case of an overweight pony, or in managing a pony suffering from laminitis. If you are doing a lot of work in the winter you may want to clip your pony and keep him in a stable at night with a rug on, turning him out with a New Zealand rug on during the day. It is really a case of working out a routine that suits both you and your pony.

ROLLING IS GOOD FOR HORSES AND THEY ALSO SEEM TO ENJOY IT.

A SHELTER WILL HELP PROTECT YOUR PONY FROM BAD WEATHER AND FLIES IN SUMMER.

PONIES ENJOY GRAZING AS THEY ARE NATURAL FORAGERS.

Pasture management

FIELDS NEED MAINTENANCE TO PROVIDE GOOD QUALITY GRAZING. TOO MANY WEEDS CAN CAUSE PROBLEMS.

A little time and effort looking after your field will be well invested. It is important that it provides a good quality of grazing, but is not too rich. Neither should it be full of weeds, wet or boggy. A small paddock can quickly become over-grazed and sour. Ponies can be fussy eaters and wasteful when they are grazing. Droppings make parts of the field unpalatable, and, as ponies browse about looking for tasty bits of grass, they tend to trample on the rest. Topping (or mowing) the field will make the grass more attractive and will tidy it up considerably. Sheep and bullocks are useful to graze the field occasionally, as they eat grass that has been rejected by ponies and help to reduce the burden of worm parasites which are not a problem to them, but can be dangerous to your pony. The field will benefit from being

REMOVE DROPPINGS FROM THE FIELD REGULARLY.

divided in two or three sections so that one section can be rested to prevent it becoming 'horse-sick'. If the field is large enough, one part could be left to grow to make hay for the winter. If you divide the field up this way, electric fencing is a useful, as it is easy to move (see page 59), but make sure the pony still has access to shelter and water.

You will help preserve the condition of the pasture by removing droppings every couple of days, and making sure that stale patches don't develop. If this is not possible, the field can be harrowed at intervals to spread the droppings.

DOCK LEAVES INDICATE THAT THE QUALITY OF THE PASTURE IS POOR.

THICK HEDGES MAKE AN EXCELLENT NATURAL FENCE.

SLACK WIRE IS A HAZARD AS HORSES CAN BECOME ENTANGLED IN IT.

Fencing, gates and field safety

A STOUT WOODEN FENCE FOR AN EXERCISE RING.

Whatever method of fencing you choose, it needs to be secure, stable and high enough. The grass is always greener on the other side, and ponies do have a tendency to escape. They need different fencing to other animals because they are more prone to injuring themselves or jumping free. Where fencing has been damaged it must be properly repaired immediately, as some ponies will take every opportunity that arises. Try to remove hazards around the field, including scrap iron, old farm machinery and any large or sharp stones. Stagnant ponds must also be fenced off as they are dangerous.

THIS POOR FENCING HAS SHARP EDGES AND IS NOT SECURE.

A WELL-MADE POST AND RAIL FENCE.

Post and rail fencing

This is the ideal. It is expensive to erect and needs to be well maintained, but it does last a long time if well looked after.

THICK, HIGH HEDGES KEEP THESE PONIES CONTAINED.

Hedges

These are suitable if they are thick and well maintained. Regular trimming will help to thicken them and keep them tidy. A good thick hedge will provide shelter from the wind and rain in winter and some shade in the summer. Hedges can become thin in winter so you need to make sure a pony doesn't push through any gaps or weak patches. Watch out for yew and deadly nightshade in a hedge. (see page 61).

BARBED WIRE FENCING.

Barbed wire

This is very dangerous and can be the cause of nasty wounds. It should be avoided at all times. Plain strands of wire are satisfactory if kept tight and if the bottom strand is at least 30 cm (1 ft) off the ground so a pony cannot get a foot over it when grazing close to the fence.

Stone walls

Common in some parts of the country, these are a good method of fencing if well maintained as they provide a natural wind-break.

Electric fencing

This has its place and ponies soon learn to respect it. It is easy to put up and move around, so it is useful for dividing up a field. Electrified tape is available in various widths from some agricultural merchants. It is much more visible to the pony than just plain wire, and he is less likely to run into it when galloping about.

HORSES SOON LEARN TO RESPECT ELECTRIC FENCING.

Gates

GATES SHOULD BE STRONG, WELL-MAINTAINED, AND HUNG CORRECTLY.

All gates should be of strong construction, sturdy and well-hung. Gates are best situated well away from a corner of the field as ponies tend to gather around when a visitor or food are expected, and arguments can develop, ending with one or more ponies getting kicked. If you are creating a new gateway, choose a well-drained part of the field so that it does not get too boggy in winter with all the traffic. For obvious safety reasons, it is best not to have a gate that opens out onto a road. Old iron gates may have sharp edges and are best avoided. The fastenings must be pony-proof so that they cannot undo them.

Poisonous plants

Some plants are very dangerous to ponies and should be removed from a field immediately. Make sure you dig them up completely (or they may grow back), and burn them. It is worth your while learning to recognize plants that can be a threat. You will find them in the pasture and in the hedgerow and they include:

- Boxwood
- Foxglove
- Green bracken
- Hellebore
- Hemlock
- Henbane
- Horsetail
- Laburnum
- Meadow saffron
- Monkshood
- Nightshade
- Oak
- Poison ivy
- Privet
- Ragwort
- Rhododendron
- Yew

RAGWORT MUST BE DUG UP (TO COMPLETELY REMOVE THE WHOLE PLANT) AND BURNT — BUT NOT IN THE HORSE'S FIELD.

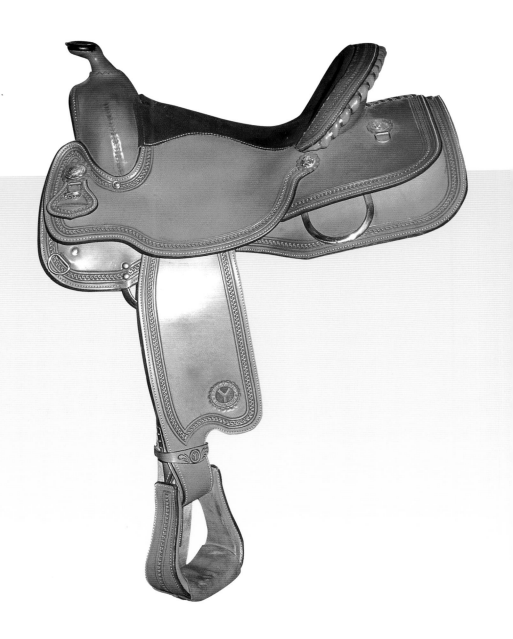

Tack and Equipment

Saddles and accessories

A saddle helps to keep you secure while riding and helps to keep your legs in the proper position. It also helps to spread a rider's weight evenly over a pony's back, keeping pressure away from its spine. Saddles are usually made of leather, although they can also be synthetic. Synthetic saddles are lightweight, which makes them easier to carry, and are easy to clean. Saddles are expensive and you should aim for the best quality saddle you can afford. If you buy a second-hand one be very wary of the stitching and general condition. A good saddle will last a lifetime, unless the pony grows out of it or you change your pony. You should look after it well, checking regularly for signs of wear and tear.

A saddle, even a new one, has to be well fitted or it will damage a pony's back. It should sit evenly and comfortably, and should not wobble about when the pony walks. You should be able to see daylight underneath the gullet when the rider is sitting on it and there should not be any pinching on the pony's body. The underside should not be lumpy and the tree and general condition of the leather and stitching should be checked carefully when buying. A saddler will usually come and check that a saddle fits the pony. Saddles are easily scratched and damaged if not put away correctly. Invest in a purpose-made saddle rack and fix it on the wall of the tack room at a height you can easily reach. Some of them have a hook underneath to hang the bridle on. If you need to stand your saddle against the wall as a temporary measure, use the girth to protect the front arch and cantle from being scratched.

TACK SHOULD BE WELL-MAINTAINED AND REPAIRED PROFESSIONALLY WHEN NECESSARY.

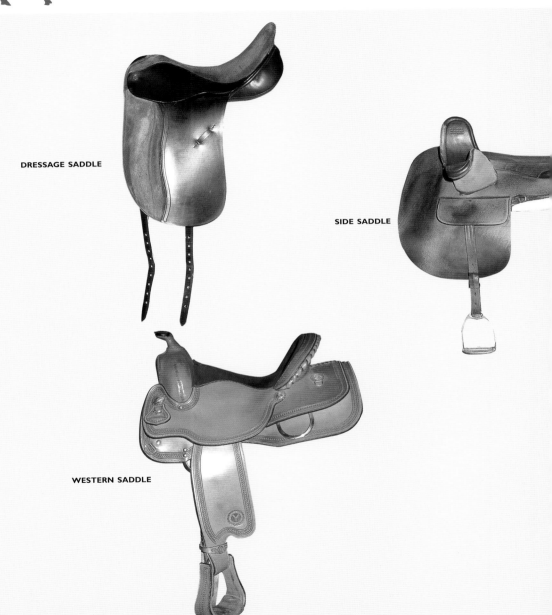

DRESSAGE SADDLE

SIDE SADDLE

WESTERN SADDLE

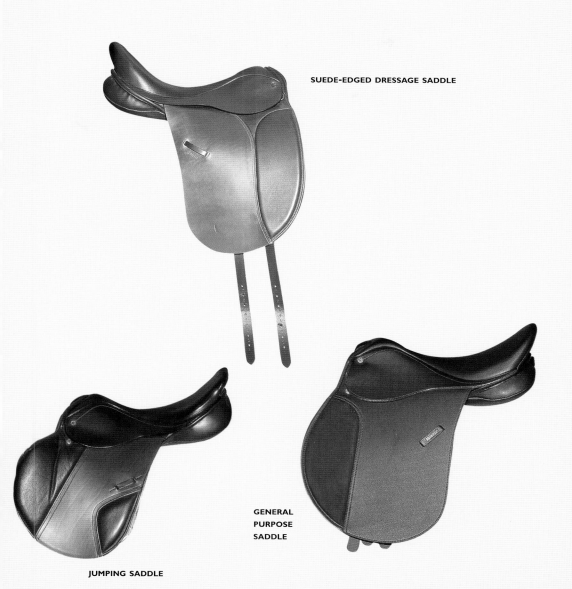

SUEDE-EDGED DRESSAGE SADDLE

**GENERAL
PURPOSE
SADDLE**

JUMPING SADDLE

The Saddle

SADDLE HORSE.

Saddle tree

The tree is the frame inside the saddle, usually made of wood or plastic. Different saddles suit different activities, for example, there are western saddles, jumping saddles, dressage saddles and eventing saddles. For general riding, you need a general purpose saddle.

Numnah

The numnah is the pad or cloth that goes under the saddle, sometimes cut to the shape of the saddle, which is used to make the pony more comfortable. They can be made of different materials, including sheepskin, which is usually the most expensive. Numnahs have various straps to secure them to a saddle. Make sure a numnah is put on correctly, and never use one to compensate for an ill-fitting saddle.

Stirrup bar

Under the skirt of a saddle is the stirrup bar. The stirrup leathers are attached to this, and the stirrups hang from the leathers. The stirrup bar is open at one end so that, if the rider were to get caught up in something, the stirrup leather would come free, instead of the rider being dragged along with the pony. Some stirrup bars have a device at the end, which can be turned upwards to stop the stirrup leather from coming off when the pony is being led without its rider. You should never ride with the bars in this position.

Stirrup leathers

These hold the stirrup onto the stirrup bar. They are made of ordinary leather or hide, or are synthetic. They tend to stretch a bit, especially when new, so always check that the holes are level or you could be riding with one stirrup longer than the other. Check the leathers regularly for rotten stitching and for signs of wear and tear.

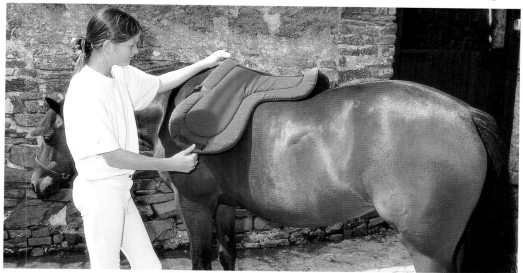

A SADDLE SHAPED NUMNAH.

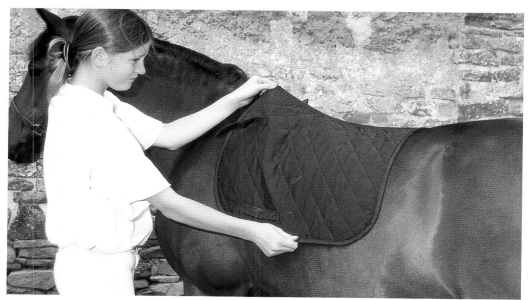

NUMNAHS VARY IN SIZE AND THICKNESS.

Stirrups

The stirrup should be approximately 1 cm. ($^1/_2$ in.) wider than the widest part of the foot. Rubber treads can be fitted to the irons to stop

CHECK STIRRUP LEATHERS BEFORE EVERY RIDE, AND CLEAN THEM REGULARLY.

the feet from slipping. It is important that children do not ride with adult stirrup irons as the whole foot can slip through with frightening consequences. Old stirrup irons made of nickel are dangerous because they may bend around the foot in an accident and crush it.

Safety stirrups

If your saddle does not have an open-ended stirrup bar, you should use safety stirrups. These have a rubber band on the side, which allows the foot to be released. Another type of safety stirrup is all metal and hinged at the top. Make sure the hinged side or rubber band is on the outside.

Girth

This is the strap that goes under the pony's stomach, just behind the forelegs, to keep the saddle in place. It is very important that it is safe and secure. Girths come in a wide variety of size, shape and colour and are commonly made of leather, webbing or nylon. Some are padded. The most important thing is that your girth is safe. Check all parts of it, including stitching, regularly and, if in any doubt, get it checked by an expert or buy a new one. Make sure you keep your girth clean, as dirt and sweat can rub and make the skin sore.

Tack

TACK SHOULD BE STORED AND PROPERLY LOOKED AFTER. ALWAYS BUY THE BEST YOU CAN AFFORD.

Tack describes the items that your pony wears for riding. It is essential that all tack fits well, is put on correctly and is looked after to ensure that it is safe to use and is not likely to break – stitching, for example, can rot eventually. Basic tack consists mainly of a saddle and a bridle. You need to learn about the different types of tack and why they may or may not be suitable for your pony. If, when you buy your pony he comes with his existing tack, it is wise to check that it is appropriate. Parts of a pony's tack may need to be replaced from time to time. He may need a different noseband or bit, for example. Always buy the best-quality tack that you can afford and, if you buy second-hand tack, take special care over the condition of the stitching and the leather. With a saddle, get the tree checked to make sure it is not broken. Tack is expensive, but should last well if looked after properly.

CHECK THE CONDITION OF SECOND-HAND TACK. WITH CAREFUL MAINTENANCE, IT SHOULD LAST WELL.

The Bridle

headpiece and goes in front of the ears to prevent the headpiece slipping backwards, and the cheek pieces, which attach the bit to the headpiece. Different nosebands are available (see page 74), but most snaffle bridles (see below) have a cavesson noseband. (see picture on page 74). Bridles without bits are used for ponies that, for some reason, are unable to hold a bit in the mouth. Most of them work by using the reins to put pressure on the nose instead of the bit. They are effective, but should only be used in experienced hands.

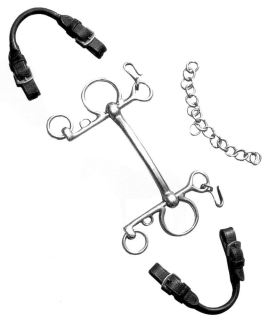

Usually made of leather, this is the set of straps (with buckles) that fit on a pony's head, and which hold the bit in his mouth. The headpiece fits behind the ears so that the throat lash, which is a part of the headpiece, does up on the near side, that is the left side as you are sitting on your pony. The throat lash helps to keep the bridle in place. Other parts of the bridle are the noseband, which fits around the nose, the brow band, which attaches to the

The bridle

This sits in the pony's mouth, on top of its tongue and between his front and back teeth. There are a huge variety of bits available – all with a different type of action on the pony's mouth. Most bits are made of stainless steel, with the part that actually goes into the mouth varying. Some are made of metal, some of rubber and some of 'vulcanite' – a kind of hardened rubber. Rubber bits are softer on the mouth than metal ones, but don't last as long. You need to check them regularly to make sure they are still in good condition. A poorly fitted bit is very uncomfortable and the mouth can

easily be damaged. You can tell when a bit has been fitted correctly because you can see a $1/2$cm ($1/4$in.) gap between the lip and the ring. A bit that does not fit will pinch. The most common type of bit is the snaffle. This may consist of loose rings, which slide through the mouthpiece, or of fixed rings as in the eggbutt snaffle. It can have either a single or double joint in the middle, or a straight bar. Pelham bits are stronger and have a curb chain. They are sometimes used on a pony that tends to be hard to stop. Check with an expert first, though – it may be your riding that needs the attention and not the bit!! Bits should always be rinsed in water after use.

SNAFFLE BIT

FOAM AROUND THE MOUTH INDICATES A COMFORTABLE BIT. NOTE THE CAVESSON NOSEBAND.

Reins

These are the straps attached to the bit which enable the rider to control a pony. They usually consist of two separate pieces of plain or plaited leather. At one end they are attached to the bit and at the other a buckle fastens them together. Some reins are partly covered with rubber for a better grip. Plain leather reins can be slippery to hold onto in the rain, or if the pony is sweaty, while plaited reins are hard to clean. Wearing gloves will give you a better grip.

Nosebands

Most ordinary snaffle bridles have a cavesson noseband (left). However, if your pony opens his mouth too wide, or crosses his jaw when being ridden, you may be advised to use a drop noseband which is worn lower than a cavesson and does up under the bit. Nosebands need to be fitted by an expert because if they are too low they can interfere with a pony's breathing. They need to be done up firmly to be effective, but not too tightly. A flash noseband is a cavesson noseband with a strap, which can be fastened under the bit to act like a drop noseband. The advantage of a flash noseband is that you can still use a standing martingale if you wish (see below), but make sure you attach it to the cavesson and not to the drop strap.

DROP NOSE BAND

Martingales

Usually made of leather, a martingale is used to stop a horse or pony from throwing its head too high in the air. Neck straps of all martingales should fasten on the near side and you should be able to get the width of your hand under them and at the withers.

Standing martingale

A standing martingale has a strap that goes between the forelegs from the girth to the noseband, and which is attached to either end with a loop. A neck strap supports this strap and a rubber ring keeps it together. Make sure you leave enough slack to allow it to push upwards to touch the throat lash.

Running martingale

A running martingale attaches to a neck strap and to the girth in the same way as a standing martingale but, as it goes through the forelegs, it divides into two with a ring at each end for the reins to go through. Rubber stops should be fitted between the rings and the bit to keep the martingale in the correct position. Again, the martingale will help prevent a pony from throwing his head too high. Care must be taken to make sure it is not fitted too tightly when attached to the girth. The rings should reach the gullet.

Irish martingale

This a small strap of leather about 10 cm (4 in.) long with a ring on each end. The reins pass through the rings and under the neck. This stops the reins being thrown over the pony's head and helps to keep them in place.

Crupper

A crupper has a padded loop which goes under the pony's tail and attaches to a ring on the back of the saddle. Its purpose is to stop the saddle from slipping forwards. Keep it clean and make sure that it does not make the tail sore.

Breast girth

This can be used to stop the saddle slipping backwards. A strap goes across the breast and attaches to the girth straps under the saddle flaps. Another strap then goes over the neck in front of the withers and holds it in place. A breast girth must not be too high or it will interfere with a pony's breathing.

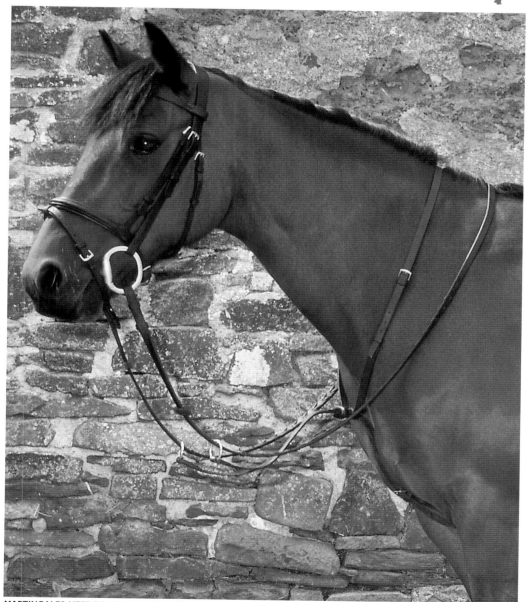

MARTINGALES NEED TO BE CORRECTLY FITTED.

STRETCHING THE LEG FORWARDS HELPS TO SMOOTH OUT ANY UNCOMFORTABLE CREASES UNDER THE GIRTH.

How to put tack on

It is important that your tack fits your pony properly and that it is well-maintained. It is vital to fasten it correctly every time you put it on and to remove it in the correct manner. A simple mistake such as not tightening the girth sufficiently will make the saddle slip. Not only will the rider fall off, but it may well frighten the pony, too – disaster!

Putting on the saddle

1 Tie your pony up, talking to him as you approach. You usually put a saddle on from the near side (the left side of the pony) so, with your left hand under the front arch and your right hand under the cantle, place the saddle on your pony's back, well forward on the withers.

2 Then gently slide it backwards into the correct position. Go round to the other side to let the girth hang down. Always go in front of your pony and not behind, in case you get kicked.

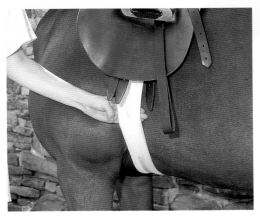

5 Make sure the girth is not twisted and that the numnah is well up into the gullet. Do not fasten the girth too tightly. Many ponies puff out their bellies when you first do up the girth so check it and perhaps tighten it by another hole or two in a couple of minutes.

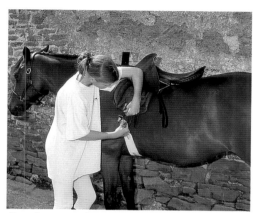

3 Return to the near side and do up the girth. Make sure the back and girth areas are clean before putting the saddle on, as dirt and sweat will rub and cause sores.

4 The buckles must be level and you should be able to insert your hand under the girth when tightened. Stand close to the shoulder when fastening the girth.

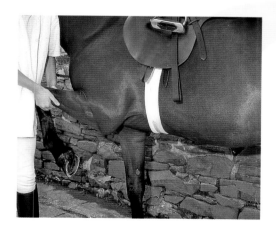

6 Pull the buckle guards down over the buckles to protect the saddle flap. Remember to check and tighten the girth again before you mount. Leave the stirrup irons run up until you are ready to mount. Stretching the leg forward evens out any creases in the skin under the girth and prevents pinching.

REMOVING SADDLE

A CRUPPER STOPS THE SADDLE SLIPPING FORWARD.

Tacking up using a martingale

If you are using a running or standing martingale, put this on before the saddle and attach the martingale to the girth.

Tacking up using a crupper

Put the crupper on after the saddle is on and the girth is done up. Stand by the hind leg on the near side and pass the tail gently through the loop of the crupper. Make sure that all the hairs are flat and comfortable and the crupper is right at the top of the tail. Attach the crupper to the metal ring on the back of the saddle, firmly enough to stop the saddle slipping forwards, but not so tight that it pulls on the tail.

A THIN STRAP UNDER THE BIT HELPS TO PREVENT THE PONY OPENING HIS MOUTH TO AVOID THE BIT.

Putting on the bridle

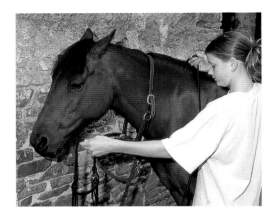

1 If you are in the stable, remove the head collar and put it away. If you are outside with your pony tied up then slip the head collar off his nose and fasten it around his neck.

2 Standing on the pony's near side, and facing forwards, put the reins over his head.

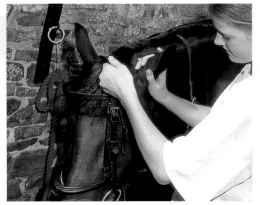

3 Pass your right hand under his chin and back over the top of his nose and hold the bridle as shown.

4 With your left hand, guide the bit into the pony's mouth, raising your right hand slightly to keep the bit in place.

5 Then put the headpiece over the ears, making sure the mane and forelock are not caught up under the bridle.

6 Do up the throatlash, so that you can get the width of your hand between the pony's cheek and the strap.

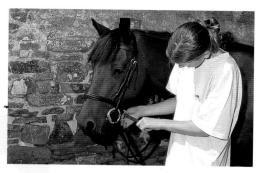

7 Do up the noseband, (attaching the martingale if used) so that you can still get two fingers under it.

8 Make sure all buckles are done up properly and that no straps are left flapping.

If you are using a running martingale or an Irish martingale, unbuckle the reins to pass the rings through and buckle them up again.

Stand in front and check that the noseband, bridle and bit all look level and comfortable.

Removing the bridle

Undo the noseband and throat lash, and slip them over the pony's ears, being careful not to bang his teeth as the bit comes out of the mouth. Put the head collar on and take the reins over the pony's head. Tie up the pony if required.

Cleaning tack

Many pony owners do not relish the thought of cleaning tack. However, maintaining your tack correctly is extremely important, and is a good time to check for signs of wear and tear. Pay particular attention to stitching, as this tends to rot and give way quicker than the leather itself. Check stirrup leathers as well and shorten them occasionally to avoid continuous wear in one place. Check the tree of the saddle periodically and be careful not to drop a saddle, which can damage the tree. Wipe your tack clean every time you go for a ride and rinse the bit.

The following procedure for cleaning tack should be carried out every week.

You Will Need:
Old cloths
Sponges
Saddle soap and oil
Clean rags
Metal polish
Dandy brush
Bucket of lukewarm water
A match or a nail

ALWAYS USE A DAMP CLOTH OR SPONGE TO CLEAN THE BRIDLE AND TACK — NEVER SUBMERGE THEM IN WATER.

How to clean a bridle

Undo all of the buckles and take the bridle apart. Using a sponge and lukewarm water, clean all parts of the bridle to remove the dirt and grease. Never soak the parts or submerge them in buckets of water. Be careful not to use hot water, which will dry out the leather by removing its natural oils. Wipe over all parts of the bridle with a cloth to remove excess water and leave to dry naturally. You do not need to oil your bridle every time you use it, but be aware that it can dry out and lose its suppleness. When you do oil, use a sponge or small paintbrush and dab oil on the underside of the leather only, which is the absorbent part. Leave the leather to soak in the oil.

Next, apply the saddle soap, making sure you follow the manufacturer's instructions. It usually comes in a bar, a tube or as a spray. If you are using a bar, dip it into the water and rub on a dry sponge. With a tube of saddle soap, apply it with a damp sponge but make sure the sponge does not become too wet. Spray soaps can be sprayed straight onto the leather. Rub soap over both sides of the leather, making sure you clean well around all the buckles and bends. Any holes that still have soap in them can be poked through with a matchstick or a nail.

When you have put the bridle back together you can give it a final wipe with saddle soap and a sponge, to remove any fingerprints. To clean the bit, wash with lukewarm water, and clean the rings with metal polish. Be sure to keep the polish away from the mouthpiece, which should only be washed with warm water. Martingales and other leather items can be cleaned in the same way as the bridle.

WIPE OFF EXCESS MOISTURE AND LEAVE TO DRY.

How to clean a leather saddle

Put your saddle on a saddle horse. Remove the stirrups and leathers, girth and girth guards, and clean the underneath with lukewarm water. Dry with a cloth and apply oil and soap in the same way as to the bridle. To dry the saddle, stand it up with something soft under the front arch for protection.

Put the saddle back on the saddle horse and clean all of the leather in the same way as you cleaned the bridle. Only apply oil to the rough underside, as oil on the seat or saddle flaps may come off on your clothes. Clean any metal with the metal polish, being very careful not to get any on the leather.

APPLY OIL TO THE UNDERSIDE ONLY — NOT ON THE SEAT OR SADDLE FLAPS..

To clean the stirrup irons, wash them with the treads removed — an old toothbrush is useful for this. Clean the treads separately. Use metal polish on the metal and replace the treads when they are dry.

Stirrup leathers are washed, oiled and soaped in the same way as the bridle. Use a matchstick to remove the soap from any holes and remember to check the stitching. How you clean the girth depends on the material it is made of.

THIS IS A GOOD TIME TO CHECK STITCHING AND SIGNS OF WEAR.

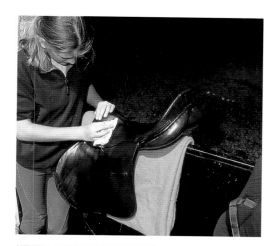

NEVER SOAK YOUR SADDLE WITH WATER.

CLEAN THE SADDLE THROUGHLY.

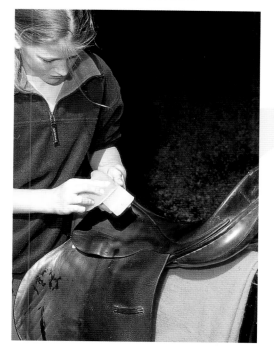

APPLY SADDLE SOAP OVER THE SADDLE.

Leather girths can be cleaned in the same way as the bridle. Webbing and padded girths should be vigorously brushed off with a dandy brush after each use and washed regularly. Follow the manufacturer's instructions for cleaning numnahs, and make sure they are kept clean and dry.

Some cotton girths can be machine-washed. Simply place a pillowcase over the buckles. To clean synthetic saddles, wipe them over with lukewarm water and a sponge. Sometimes a mild detergent can be used, but follow the manufacturer's instructions.

Boots

A wide range of boots are available to protect a
pony's legs from knocks and injuries while
being ridden and during travel. Some of the
boots used while exercising prevent the pony
getting injured, while others, such as brushing
boots, for example, prevent him injuring himself,
and are used for general riding (see below and
picture, right).

All-in-one travel boots

These cover from above the knee or hock down
to the coronet band. They are quick and easy to
fit and provide good protection. Alternatively,
you could use stable bandages with padding
underneath (see the picture on page 93).

Brushing boots

Fitted below the knee, these protect the pony
from any injury should he strike himself with
another foot or leg while being ridden.
Sometimes a rubber ring with a strap through its
centre is fitted just above a pony's fetlock to
serve the same purpose. Some people use
brushing boots on all four legs, others just on
the front legs. Different ponies have different
confirmation and action, which makes some of
them more prone to injuring themselves than
others. Brushing boots should be fitted firmly

BRUSHING BOOTS PROTECT THE HORSE FROM SELF-INFLICTED INJURY WHILE BEING RIDDEN.

but not too tightly, and with no mud
underneath, which make him sore. Speedycut
boots are similar to brushing boots, but are
fitted a little higher up.

Overreach boots

These are similar to a bell in shape and are
made of rubber. They protect the heel and
coronet of the fore feet and fit around the
pastern. Some have Velcro straps but most are
the type you pull over the hoof to fit them,
which is not always easy. Turn each boot inside
out to pull it over the hoof, then fold it down to
cover the coronet and heel. Keep a check on
the pasterns to make sure the boots are not
rubbing. Overreach boots are used while
exercising and travelling to prevent injuries to
the coronet and heel should the pony tread on
himself with his hind feet. They have a tendency
to turn upwards and inside out, especially while
riding in muddy conditions, which could trip a
pony up.

Tendon boots

Used only on the front legs, these prevent
injuries to the tendon area if the horse should
strike himself quite high up with his hind foot.
They have a thick pad that runs down the back
of the leg. Often tendon and brushing boots are

combined in one. Tendon boots do not support
the tendons.

Knee boots

These are mostly used to protect the knees while
travelling. Knocks can occur while loading and
unloading or in an accident. Knee boots are
also used during exercise, however these are
often referred to as skeleton kneepads. These
consist of a hard pad to protect the knee should
the horse fall on his knees, particularly on the
road. Both types have a padded strap around
the top which should be fastened firmly, but not
too tight, and strap around the bottom which
should be loose enough not to interfere with the
movement of the leg.

Hock boots

Used to protect the point of the hock, these are
usually used against knocks and bumps while
travelling. They have a hard pad to cover the
point of the hock and a strap above and below
the hock to secure them. Fit the boots as you do
for the knee boots.

Yorkshire boots

These are very simple and are effective as a
brushing boot for some ponies. They are simply
a rectangular piece of material, usually felt, with

a tape sewn across the middle. It is wrapped around the leg with the tape on the outside, and tied just above the fetlock. You then fold down the top half of the boot giving a double layer of protection.

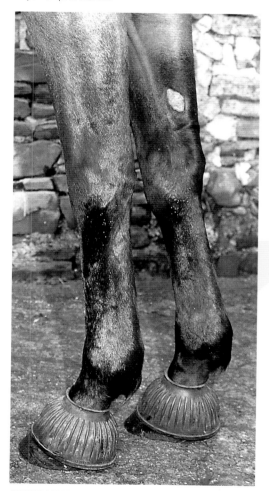

OVERREACH BOOTS PROTECT THE FRONT LEGS.

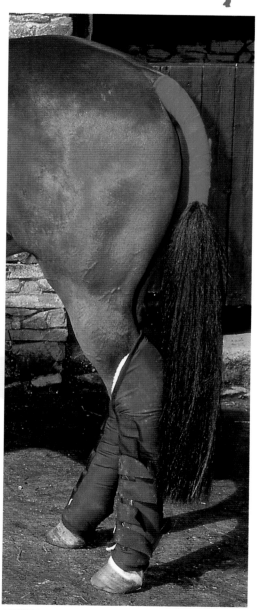

TRAVELLING BOOTS ARE EASY TO PUT ON.

Bandages

Used in first aid, during exercise, when travelling or in the stable, bandages have various uses. They must be put on correctly, however. Too loose, and they become ineffective. They could slip and cause an accident. Too tight, and they could actually cause an injury, interfering with a pony's circulation. Never sit on the floor or kneel when fitting a bandage, but squat down. This way you will be able to move away much quicker should you need to.

Exercise bandages

Usually about 7 cm (3 in.) wide and approximately 150 cm (6 ft) long these have a cotton tape to secure them. They must be put on correctly and it is probably safer to use brushing boots if you are inexperienced at bandaging. Use padding underneath the bandage for comfort and protection against knocks. Make sure any padding is smooth and without creases when fitted. Exercise bandages are made of slightly stretchy fabric, such as crepe, which is easy to put on too tight. If they get wet during exercise remove them immediately as they tend to tighten even more when wet. These bandages reach from just below the knee or hock to just above the fetlock

and must not be allowed to interfere with any of these joints.

Stable bandages

Made of wool or stockinet, stable bandages are wider and longer than exercise bandages. They are used when travelling and in the stables, and can also be used to bandage ponies' legs when they become wet and muddy. They will help to dry them off and will reduce chapping. They also offer protection from knocks when travelling.

Using a bandage

To put on a stable bandage, wrap the padding around the leg making sure it is not creased anywhere. Then start to bandage just below the knee or hock and wrap around the leg passing the bandage from one hand to the other making sure you keep the tension even until you reach the coronet. Continue back up the leg to the beginning.

Tie a bow on the outside of the leg and tuck the tapes in so they can't get caught on anything. A knot tied at the back of the leg will press on the tendons and should be avoided. When removing bandages, do so quickly and quietly passing from one hand to the other.

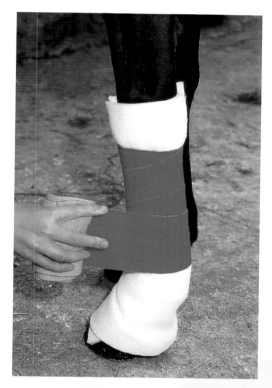

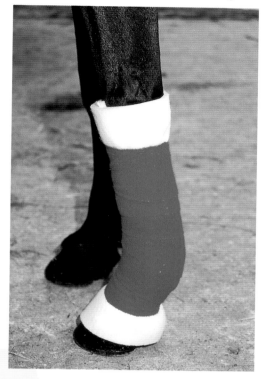

MAKE SURE THE PADDING DOES NOT CREASE UNDER THE BANDAGE. APPLY WITH EVEN PRESSURE ALL THE WAY DOWN

STABLE BANDAGES ARE VERSATILE AND AN ESSENTIAL ITEM FOR YOUR TACK ROOM.

Never try to roll the bandage up while you are removing it, do that later. After use, wash and dry the bandage if necessary and put away for the next time. To roll the bandage, fold up the tapes and start with the outside edge upwards.

Roll the bandage up with your hand until you reach the end. If a bandage is not rolled up correctly, you will have to re-roll it before use next time. Practice bandaging when you have spare time and you will soon improve.

When you tie the tape at the end of applying the bandage make sure it is not too tight. You can go over the cotton tape with masking tape if you are worried about it coming undone while you are riding.

Tail bandages

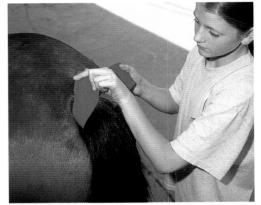

1. Tail bandages are used while travelling, to prevent a pony from rubbing his tail, and after grooming, to encourage the hair to lie flat. To apply, dampen the top of the tail with a water brush.

2. Pass the end of the bandage under the top of the tail and wind it round once, leaving a small flap sticking up. This gets folded down as you wind around the second time.

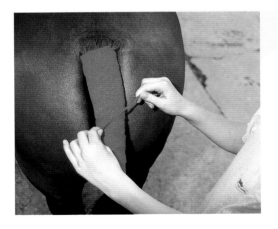

3. Never put a tail bandage on too tight, as this could injure the bone. If the hairs become severely damaged, they may grow back white.

 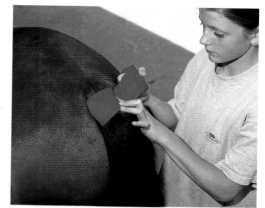

3 Wind all the way to the end of the tail bone keeping an even pressure all the way. Then wind back upwards until you run out of bandage, which should be about two-thirds of the way back up.

4 Tie the tapes making sure you keep them flat. Tie a double bow and tuck the ends in. Gently shape the tail.

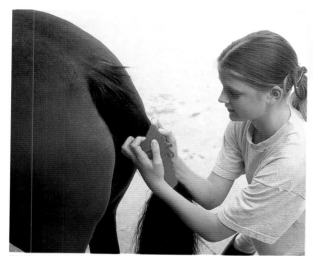

TO REMOVE, PULL THE WHOLE BANDAGE DOWN FROM THE TOP, AND WIND UP LATER.

Horsecare

Grooming

Most ponies enjoy being groomed and it is an ideal time to get to know your pony and check over his general health and condition. Grooming not only makes your pony look neat and tidy, but also helps keep his skin healthy. If you put lots of energy into grooming, you can even improve a pony's muscle tone and circulation. This type of grooming is called 'strapping' and is normally done to stabled horses and ponies. Then, when you want to exercise them, a quick brush over will be adequate. This is called 'quartering'. Ponies at grass will need different grooming routines depending on their lifestyle. A few ponies are ticklish, so try to brush fairly firmly. Grooming machines are used in some large yards, but for most of us, a well-equipped grooming kit and lots of elbow grease will have to do!

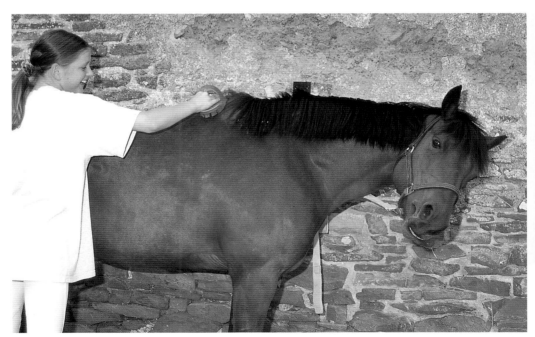

GROOMING IS AN EXCELLENT WAY OF BONDING WITH YOUR PONY.

Equipment in a grooming kit

KEEP YOUR GROOMING KIT IN A SPECIAL BOX SO IT'S READY WHEN YOU NEED IT.

Your grooming kit should be kept in a suitable box – one with a handle is useful. It is important to keep all your equipment clean and tidy or you won't have all your kit together when you need it. Wash your brushes on a sunny day and leave them out to dry.

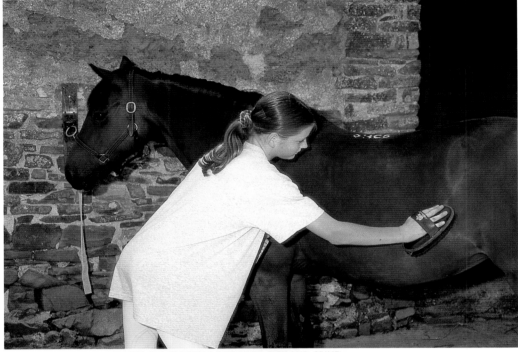

A BODY BRUSH ALLOWS YOU TO REACH DEEPLY INGRAINED DIRT AND GRIME.

Dandy brush

A large brush with stiff, long bristles, it is used for caked-on mud, particularly on grass-kept ponies. A dandy brush should not be used on the face or the tail as it is too harsh.

Body brush

This has shorter, denser bristles and enables you to get deeper into the skin to remove dirt, scurf and grease.

Water brush

This looks similar to a dandy brush but has softer and shorter hairs. It is used to damp down the mane and tail when plaiting or grooming, and will make the hair lie flat. It is also used to wash and scrub the feet.

Curry comb

There are three types of curry comb: a metal one is used to scrape the body brush to get it clean. It has very sharp serrated edges and

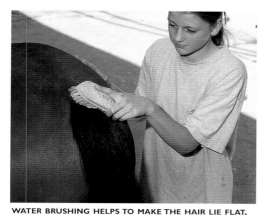

WATER BRUSHING HELPS TO MAKE THE HAIR LIE FLAT.

caked-on mud. Avoid using curry combs on a pony's face.

Mane comb

A plastic or metal comb with teeth used to comb manes. It is best avoided on the tail as it tends to pull out hair.

should never be used on a pony's body. Rubber and plastic curry combs are good for getting excess hair out of the coat, and for removing

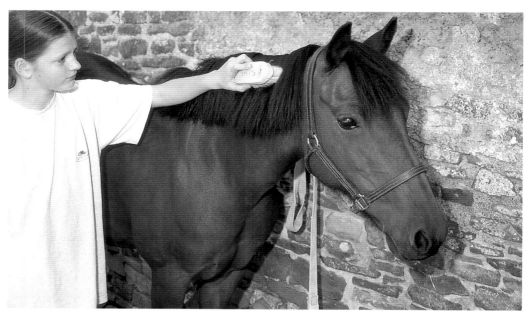

AS A FINISHING TOUCH, USE A DAMP WATER BRUSH ON THE MANE TO ENCOURAGE THE HAIR TO LIE FLAT.

OILING THE HOOVES AT THE END OF A GROOMING SESSION.

Hoof oil and brush

Use a brush on the hooves. Leave oiling until the end of a grooming session or it will end up with dust and dirt stuck all over it.

Stable rubber

This can simply be a tea towel or a glass cloth, and is used to give a final polish and to remove any surface dust.

Sponge

You will need three sponges, one for the eyes, one for the nostrils and one for the dock. It is a good idea to label them to avoid confusion.

Sweat scraper

This has a handle and a semi- circular rubber blade to scrape off excess water.

Shampoo

There are a variety of horse shampoos available. Aways use a proper equine shampoo rather than a human variant, as this will avoid irritating your pony's skin.

Hoof pick

This is used to clean stones and mud out of the feet.

Grooming a stabled pony

Take your kit to the stable, put the head collar on your pony, and tie him up. Leave the door open so you have more light. Place the water buckets outside so they don't fill with dirt. Start by picking out the feet. Facing the tail, lift one foot and, holding the hoof in your inside hand, use your outside hand to scrape the hoof pick from the heel towards the toe. Never scrape in the opposite direction, or you could hurt the frog or the heel. Lower the hoof without dropping it and repeat for the remaining feet. As you go, look out for any bad smell, which could be a sign of thrush (see page 173). This is also a good time to check that the pony's shoes are secure. If you have one, you can save time by picking the feet out over a bowl or bucket.

PICKING OUT THE FEET INTO A BOWL SAVES SWEEPING THE YARD LATER!

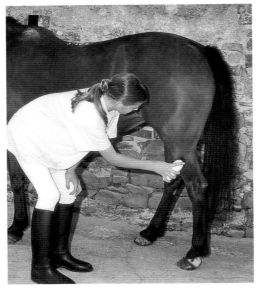

USE A DANDY BRUSH TO REMOVE SWEAT OR MUD.

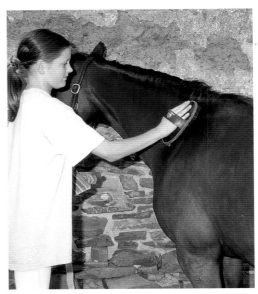

A SOFTER BODY BRUSH REMOVES DEEPER GRIME.

SCRAPE OFF THE BODY BRUSH ON A CURRY COMB.

TAP THE COMB ON THE FLOOR TO REMOVE THE DIRT.

Take the dandy brush and, starting behind the ears, use it to remove any mud or sweat marks. Be careful on sensitive parts of the body and don't use at all on any clipped parts. Pay attention to the hocks, as these tend to get dirty when the pony is lying down in the stable.

Take the body brush and the metal curry comb. You will need to use both hands now. Start behind the ears again and brush down the neck, making sure you get right under the mane. Brush in the direction of the coat and lean into the brush a little as you do so. After about three strokes with the brush, pull it across the metal curry comb to remove mud and grease.

To remove dirt and grease from the curry comb, tap it on the stable floor occasionally. You will accumulate quite a pile, even from a pony that looked clean to start with. When you have brushed both sides, move on to the head. Remove the head collar and brush the head very gently.

Lastly, run your fingers through the pony's mane to remove any large tangles. then brush through with the body brush.

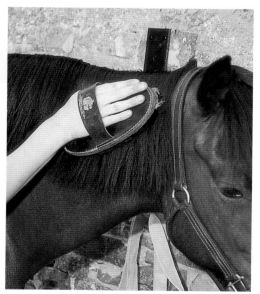

USING A PLASTIC COMB TO REMOVE DUST.

USE A SOFT BRUSH ON THE MANE.

USE SEPARATE SPONGES FOR EYES, NOSE AND DOCK.

GENTLY SPONGE THE PONY'S FACE.

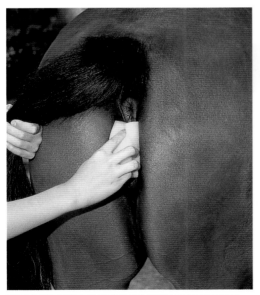

WASH THE DOCK TO MAKE THE PONY COMFORTABLE.

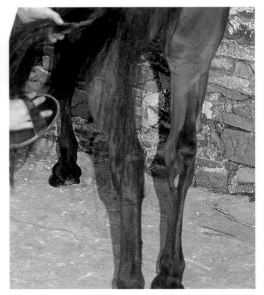

WITH A SOFT BRUSH, COMB A FEW HAIRS AT A TIME.

Sponge the eyes, nostrils and dock using the different sponges. Always wash the sponges in plain water, and wring each one out well. When wiping the eyes, start in the corner and wipe outwards. When washing the dock, be careful to stand to one side, so that you don't get kicked. Lift the tail and gently sponge the whole area, remembering to clean the underside of the tail as well.

Take the body brush again and, after removing the worst of the tangles in the tail with your fingers, brush through the tail, a section at a time. Hold the rest of the tail in one hand and stand to one side to avoid getting kicked or trodden on should the pony take a step backwards. You can use a tail bandage to make the tail hairs stay flat for longer. Dampen the water brush, shake it, and brush the mane and the top of the tail to flatten them.

Wipe the whole pony with a slightly damp stable rubber or cloth to remove any last bits of dust. Lastly, using the brush and oil, paint the hooves. Do not use too much oil and be careful not to get any of it on the white hair of the coronet. Opinions vary on whether or not to use oil every day.

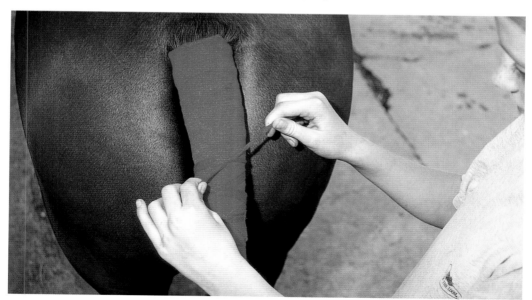

USE A TAIL BANDAGE TO MAKE THE TAIL HAIRS REMAIN FLAT.

Quartering

This is a quicker method of grooming and is often used on a stabled horse before exercise, although he will also have a thorough 'strapping' later. Leave the rug on a pony, undoing just the front strap, and brush over the pony quickly to remove any stable stains. Fold the back half of the rug forwards to brush the back half of the pony, and vice versa. Pick out the feet, and sponge eyes, nostrils and dock.

Grooming a grass-kept pony

Grooming a pony that is out at grass takes less time, but is still an important part of his day. It is also a good time for you to check him over for any problems. Pick out the feet and sponge the eyes, nostril and dock. Use the dandy brush to remove any mud. If there is mud on the pony's head pick it off with your fingers and

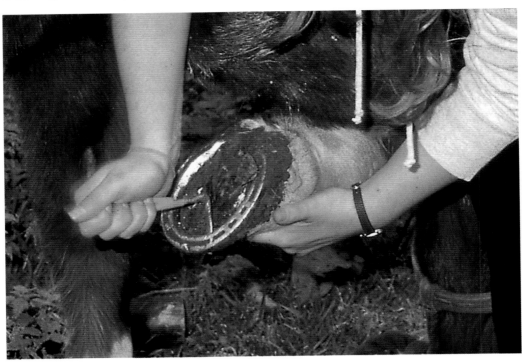

REMOVING MUD FROM A HOOF.

then use a body brush on the mane and tail once you have removed the worst of the tangles with your fingers. If the pony has grass or stains where he has rolled over, remove them with water and a sponge or a water brush. Leave these areas to dry completely before using the dandy brush. If you want to ride when it has been raining and the pony is wet, use a sweat scraper to scrape off all the excess water. Dry the saddle and bridle areas thoroughly with an old towel, and brush the pony over before riding. Even if the rest of your pony is not gleaming, he must be clean and dry under the saddle and bridle or he will become uncomfortable and get sore. Do not forget to dry the girth areas too.

REMOVE THE WORST TANGLES FROM YOUR PONY'S MANE BEFORE BRUSHING.

Bathing your pony

1 When the weather is hot, or if you are off to impress your friends at the local show, bathing your pony will make him look really smart. Some shampoos will help keep the flies away too. It is not sensible to bathe a pony in winter, when he could easily get cold or catch a chill.

2 Some ponies dislike being bathed, while others seem to enjoy the attention. If your pony is not used to being bathed, or is not keen on it, get someone experienced to help you. If a new pony is not used to water being poured over it, do it very gently and avoid getting soap in its eyes.

5 To wash the tail, stand to the side as for grooming, then dampen, shampoo and rinse well. Swish the tail around to remove excess water and start to dry it. Never stand directly behind a pony.

3 Using a hose pipe tends to frighten ponies, and they can get caught up in it. Use a small bucket or bowl instead and wet the coat with lukewarm water. Shampoo the mane and forelock and rinse thoroughly. Wash the hooves with a water brush.

4 Work over the whole body, making sure you rinse thoroughly with lukewarm water. Use the sweat scraper to remove excess water from the body.

6 When you have bathed the whole pony, you should not let him get cold. Walk him around, rub his legs, heels and head with an old towel and put on a sweat rug with another light rug on top. This will help him to keep warm while drying. Brush all over with a body brush when he is dry.

Trimming and clipping

Horses and ponies need clipping in order to remove their winter coats. Clipped ponies are not only easier to groom, but they also sweat less when working, and then dry more quickly, which helps to avoid chills. Trimming is carried out with scissors or small clippers, and tidies up any unwanted hair.

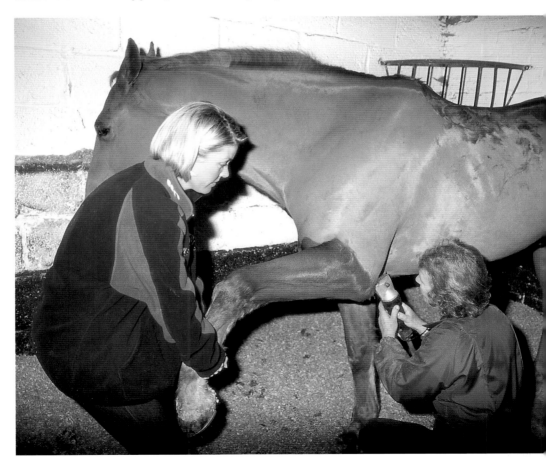

Trimming

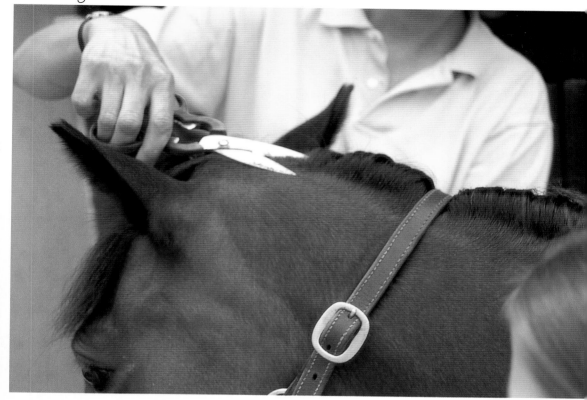

TRIMMING KEEPS YOUR PONY TIDY, BUT IS BEST CARRIED OUT BY EXPERTS.

Trimming your pony helps make him look tidy and smart, although some of the processes such as mane and tail pulling and clipping are best left to the experts. A poorly pulled mane or a bad clip will take a long time to grow out and clipping can be dangerous if you are inexperienced.

Generally, stable-kept ponies need more clipping and trimming than grass-kept ones.

Trimming can be done simply with a pair of scissors in some areas. Ponies tend to get long hairs around the jaw and under the chin, which can be removed. Be very careful with scissors

A SMALL SET OF CLIPPERS IS SOMETIMES USED ON DELICATE AREAS SUCH AS THE HEAD.

around your pony, particularly near his eyes, and always put them away as soon as you have finished. Ears should be trimmed on the outside only. Never cut any hair from inside the ears. A clever technique is to close the ear together with your hand and trim off any hair left sticking out. Do not cut off a pony's whiskers as they are there to serve a purpose. Without them your pony will not be able to judge some distances and might bump his nose on things.

The heels of a stable-kept pony can be kept trimmed all year. Use a comb to push the hair the wrong way and then cut in an upward direction. The heels of a grass-kept pony should be left untrimmed, particularly in winter when he will need protection from the wet and the mud. The long hairs of the fetlocks act as drain pipes for excess water.

Hair is sometimes removed from behind the ears so that the bridle and head collar sit better (see picture page 115). It is not always necessary, but sometimes the mane can be very thick here, so it can help to tidy it up. You will have to keep it trimmed, however, as it will look very untidy when it starts to grow. Some people also trim the mane at the withers but it is not really necessary.

'Hogging' is a term used to describe the cutting off of the whole mane using clippers. This can solve the problem of a patchy or untidy mane, but it will take up to two years to re-grow fully, so be very sure before you do it. The mane is clipped from the withers up to the poll, while the head and neck are gently stretched downwards as much as possible. This needs to be done by an expert and should be repeated every four to six weeks.

'Pulling a mane' is a means of both shortening and thinning it, which tidies up the pony and makes plaiting easier. To pull the mane, you remove the long hairs from underneath, either with your fingers, or by wrapping a few hairs at a time around a mane comb. Pulling should be done after exercise when the skin is warm and the pores are open, making it less uncomfortable for the pony. Keep pulling out the longest hairs, a few at a time along the length of the mane, until the desired length and thickness are achieved. Never take hairs from the top of the mane or it will stick up. Pulling a tail needs practice and it is sensible to watch an experienced person a few times before you attempt it yourself. Remember that the mane of a grass-kept pony helps to keep him warm in the winter, and that he needs a thick tail to

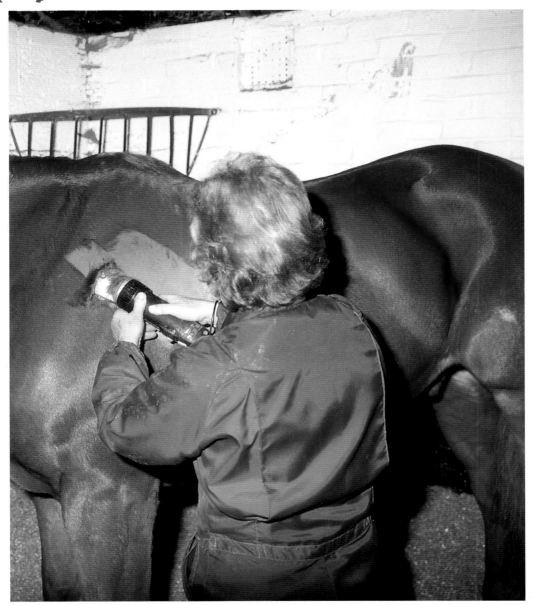

CLIPPING HAS SEVERAL BENEFITS: IT PREVENTS EXCESSIVE SWEATING AND ALLOWS THE HORSE TO DRY QUICKLY.

protect his dock area from the weather, so it should never be pulled.

To trim the tail you need to cut it straight across the bottom so that when it is carried naturally it is about 12 cm (6 in.) below the point of the hock. A long tail collects mud and looks untidy.

Horses and ponies that do hard or regular work will benefit from being clipped to various degrees. Some only need the belly and under the neck taken off – this is usually the practice on ponies – and others need a full clip where all the hair is removed. The more hair you remove, the more clothing you will need in order to keep him warm when he is not working. Clipping a hard-working horse has several advantages. It removes the winter coat, which would otherwise cause heavy sweating and could affect the animal's condition. It also enables a horse to dry off more quickly after exercise, making him less susceptible to catching a chill.

Grooming becomes much easier too. Clipping is a job for an expert and you should be able to find one by word of mouth or from an advertisement in the local paper. Clipping is usually carried out in late autumn and should be repeated every six to eight weeks until late winter. Do not clip after that time or it will interfere with the summer coat. Ponies that only do a little light hacking at the weekends and don't become too sweaty do not usually need to be clipped. In this case, particularly if he is out at grass, it would be much better to leave his winter coat intact. A New Zealand rug (see page 33) is important if even a little hair has been removed or a pony will quickly catch colds and lose condition. Never leave a clipped pony without a rug on. Once you have removed his natural coat it is your responsibility to keep him warm – anything less would be unkind.

Types of clip

Neck and belly clip: Suitable for ponies working during weekends and holidays. A pony can live out at grass with this clip if he has a good shelter and a New Zealand rug.

Chaser clip: As above.

Trace clip: Suitable for ponies in medium work, this keeps the neck warm but quite a lot of hair is removed. If you put him out in the field often, you will need to make sure he is warm enough. Most ponies would be stabled at night at least with this clip.

Hunter clip: For horses in hard work. Hair is left on the legs, to protect them from thorns and brambles, and on the saddle patch for comfort. A horse will need to be kept well rugged-up at all times. He would normally be kept stabled and, if turned out during the day, must have a good, thick New Zealand rug.

Blanket clip: The horse still has hair on the legs, back and quarters. This is best suited to horses and ponies in medium to hard work. They would normally be stabled at night at least.

Preparing to clip

Some ponies are nervous of clippers. If this is the case, talk to your pony to reassure him and stroke his neck gently. Run the clippers near him for a while to let him get used to the noise before you start. Most will accept being clipped once they are used to it. When you have found an experienced person to do the clip for you, and you have arranged a time for it to be done, you need to groom the pony thoroughly using the body brush to remove as much dirt and grease from the coat as possible. A dirty coat could blunt or overheat the clippers. Never bathe a pony the same day, as he needs to be completely dry. Use a tail bandage to keep the tail out of the way, and be ready with a stable rug (see page 33) as clipping can take a long time and the pony might start to get cold half way through.

MANE PLAITING EQUIPMENT (SEE PAGE 122).

Plaiting your pony

It's a good idea to practice plaiting so that, when that a special occasion arrives, such as a local show, you will be able to make your pony look really smart. The more you practice, the easier it will become, and the end result will be neater each time. You usually plait on the off side of the neck, and the number of plaits down the neck is traditionally odd with the one in the fore lock making it even. I find it best not to plait the night before a show because it rarely looks as neat in the morning.

1 To plait your pony you will need a body brush, a mane comb, a water brush and some plaiting bands. The pony needs to have a short mane that is not too thick. Use the body brush to brush out the mane. You can use a mane comb for the final comb-through once you have removed all the tangles, then use the water brush to dampen the mane.

4 Pass the right strand over the centre one, then the left strand over the centre one and so on until you reach the end of the hair. It is very important to keep the plait tight all the way down or it will be loose when you come to fold it. Tie a band firmly around the end so that it does not become loose.

5 You can either do all the plaits like this first and then roll them up, or roll up each one as you go along. To fold the plait, bend it in half with the end underneath and then fold in half again. Then, with a band, wind it around the bobble several times until it is tight.

2 If you don't do this you may end up with stray hairs sticking up all over the place. Divide the mane up into the number of plaits you want to end up with and secure each bunch with a band. Use the mane comb to divide the mane, making sure you get a neat, straight divide between each bunch.

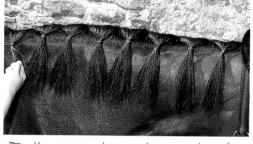

3 You may need to stand on something if you are not tall enough to get a good view of what you are doing. If you use a bucket, be careful that it is strong enough to take your weight and that the handle has been removed. Take the first bunch – it is a good idea to start at the withers' end, as some ponies are sensitive about you pulling on their manes, especially at the poll – and divide it into three equal sections.

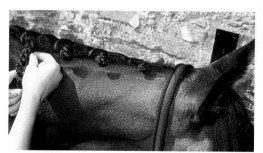

6 Plaiting bands are available in several colours so choose one as close to the colour of your pony's mane as possible. A needle and thread can be used instead of the bands, but I find bands are safer and easier. If you drop the needle, you will waste a lot of time literally searching for a needle in a haystack.

7 Try plaiting as often as possible, as practice makes perfect! And use a little hair wax to smooth and fix down any odd stray hairs for a perfect finish.

Plaiting a tail

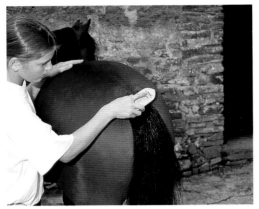

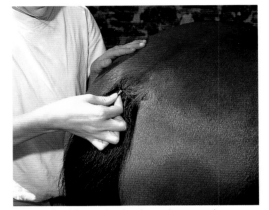

1 A well-plaited tail is very smart, but it does take practise. The tail needs to have long hairs at the top and the whole tail needs to be brushed out and clean.

2 A freshly washed tail can be very slippery to plait, so it is better to wash the tail a couple of days before the show if you can. This might not be possible if the tail is very light in colour as it will not stay clean.

5 Secure this with a band, tuck the end under the bottom of the plait and fix with another band. You can use a large needle to sew it in place but be very careful not to loose the needle.

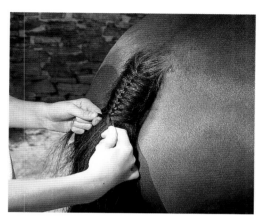

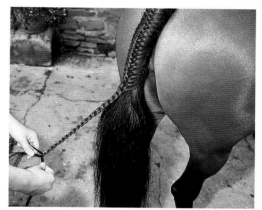

3 To plait the tail, take a few hairs from each side and secure them together with a bit of cotton the same colour as the tail. Then take a strand from each side and plait in the normal way until you reach the end of the tail bone.

4 Be careful to keep the plait tight all the way down and keep it centred – it is very easy to drift to one side. When you reach the end of the tail bone continue to plait the three strands you have in your hand until the end of the hair.

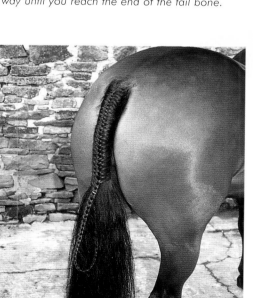

6 A little wax can be used to smooth down any stray hairs or any that were too short to be plaited. Practice will soon make perfect, so have a go at plaiting the tail whenever you have a few spare moments.

Feet and shoeing

THE FROG OF THE FOOT.

The outside of the foot consists of the wall of the hoof, the sole, which is the bottom of the foot and the frog, which is the 'V'-shaped part of the sole. The frog is like a wedge of rubber and helps cushion the foot as it is brought to the ground and prevents the pony from slipping. Together, the parts of the outer foot protect the sensitive internal structures – the nerves and bones – from injury.

Hooves grow throughout a pony's life. In the wild, ponies rely on their feet to make a quick escape if they sense danger, and they wear their feet down naturally on their continual quest for fresh food. By domesticating and riding a horse, you are changing its environment and lifestyle. This means that you also have to change the way that its feet are managed.

Daily care of the hooves must include checking for loose or lost shoes, picking out the hooves and checking for lameness or heat. If a pony is not free to roam over all types of terrain, the feet will not naturally be worn down and so will grow too long and crack. If ridden a lot on the road, on the other hand, the feet will wear down quicker than they grow and will become sore.

Shoes are needed to prevent wear on the hoof. Once shoes have been fitted they must be removed every six to eight weeks, trimmed and replaced. The same shoes can be used again if they are not worn out. Even if a pony does not need new shoes, they must still be replaced and trimmed, because the foot will have grown. Overgrown feet put a lot of strain on the joints and tendons, and can cause a pony to stumble. Other problems that might occur include a shoe becoming loose or being lost altogether, a shoe becoming thin through too much hard work, or the nails that hold the shoe beginning to stick up.

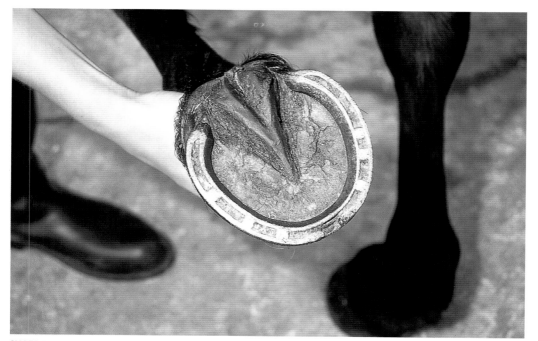

SHOES PREVENT THE HOOF FROM WEARING. THEY NEED TO BE WELL FITTED AND REPLACED EVERY **6–8** WEEKS.

FIRST, THE FARRIER REMOVES THE OLD NAILS.

THEN HE LEVERS OFF THE OLD SHOE.

THE HORN OF THE HOOF IS TRIMMED.

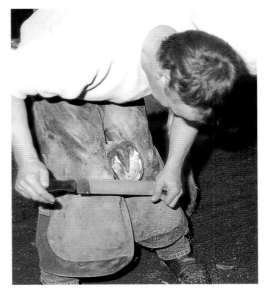

THE HOOF IS RASPED TO PREPARE FOR THE NEW SHOE.

A FARRIER SHAPING A RED HOT SHOE.

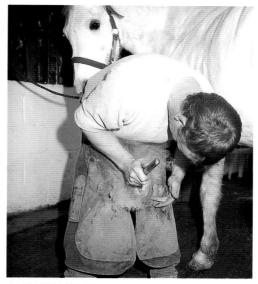

A HOT SHOE IS POSITIONED AMID MUCH SMOKE.

A farrier is very skilled and has to train for a long time before being qualified to trim and shoe ponies. No-one other than a farrier should interfere with or attempt to trim a pony's foot. Most farriers shoe 'hot' which means that they heat the shoe until it is red hot, which makes it easier to shape and enables a better fit. When a pony loses a shoe it is called 'casting a shoe'. When the same shoes are replaced once the feet have been trimmed it is called 'removes'.

Shoeing

Hot shoeing is the most common practice these days. First, an old shoe has to be removed. This is done by removing the heads from the nails (clenches) with a buffer and a hammer, and levering the shoe off with pincers.

The long horn then needs to be trimmed back with a knife. A farrier inspects all parts of the foot and rasps it in places to make a level surface ready for the new shoe.

A shoe is then made in the forge, or a ready-made shoe is altered to fit the pony. This is done by shaping the shoe on an anvil using a hammer. The hot shoe is carried to the pony on a 'pritchel' and held against the foot while it is still red hot to measure the fit. This makes a lot of smoke, and smells and looks painful, but does not hurt the pony at all. When the farrier is happy with the shape and size of the shoe it is cooled, usually by dunking it in a bucket of water, and nailed on. The nails are made especially for the job and must be the correct shape and size for the shoe. Great skill is required to make sure that the nails are driven into the correct parts of the hoof and not into the sensitive tissue causing 'pricked foot' (see page 173). There are usually four nails on the outside of the shoe and three on the inside, and the farrier usually begins at the toe. The nails are then bent over and cut off. They are then called clenches, and are then hammered down. The front shoe normally has a clip at the toe and the hind shoe has two – one on either side. These help to keep the shoe in the correct position. The hoof wall and clenches are then tided up using a rasp. Studs are used to prevent a pony from slipping and are screwed into the heel of the shoe or can be a permanent part of the shoe.

THE NEW SHOE IS NAILED ON.

THE CLENCHES ARE HAMMERED DOWN.

MOST FARRIERS ARE MOBILE AND WILL VISIT YOU.

Things to look for in a newly shod foot:

- The shoe must have been made to fit the foot and not the foot made to fit the shape of the shoe.
- The frog should be in contact with the ground.
- The hoof has been trimmed adequately to make it completely level.
- The correct number and sizes of nails have been used.
- The clip is well fitted.
- There are no gaps between the hoof wall and the shoe.
- The clenches are not sticking out and are the correct distance from the shoe.
- The correct type and weight of shoe for your requirements has been fitted.

Riding without shoes

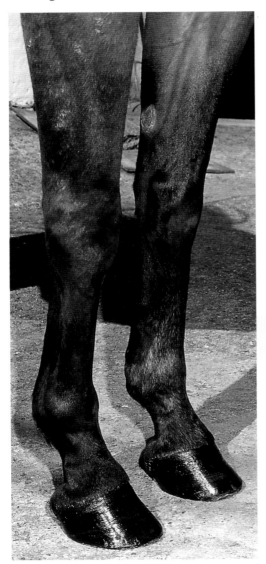

SHOES ARE NOT ALWAYS NECESSARY.

It is possible to ride without shoes, depending on how much riding you are going to do and on what type of surface you are going to ride. Frequent riding on hard or gritty roads or stony paths will not be possible without causing a pony's feet to become sore and worn down. Riding without shoes obviously saves a lot of money, but the feet still need to be kept trimmed and level. If a pony has been shod in the past, it takes a while for the feet to get used to going out without shoes. Preparations are also available which can be painted on parts of the hoof to harden it. This allows you to do a little more riding on the road than otherwise.

An un-shod pony is less likely to slip on the road and, if you are on the receiving end of a kick, you will fare much better. Some ponies benefit from shoes on the front feet even if they do not need them on the hind feet. You should not be marked down at local shows if your pony does not have shoes as long as the hooves are well trimmed.

Teeth

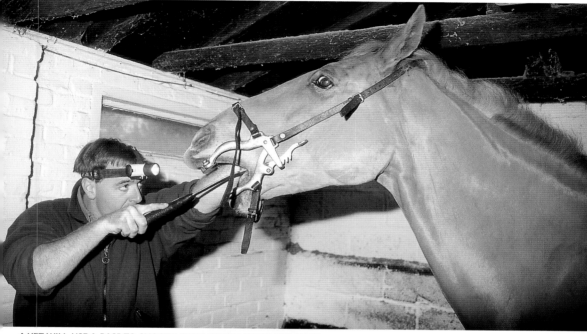

A VET WILL USE A RASP TO SMOOTH AWAY ROUGH EDGES ON TEETH.

Ponies and horses have up to 42 teeth – 12 incisors, 24 molars, 4 tushes and 2 wolf teeth. Some ponies do not develop the wolf teeth at all and mares often do not have tushes. The incisors are at the front of the mouth and are used for grazing. Next there is a gap where the tushes grow, and at the back are the molars. The molars are used to grind the food and it is these that may become sharp as the teeth wear down. If the wolf teeth are present they grow in the top of the jaw, in front of the molars, and may need to be removed as they can cause discomfort.

A pony's teeth need regular attention in order to avoid eating problems and sores in the mouth. They should be checked every six months at least. Unlike our teeth, ponies' teeth grow all the time and natural wearing sometimes leaves them uneven and with sharp

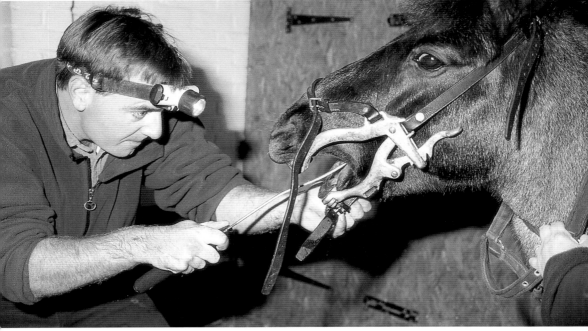

TEETH MUST BE REGULARLY CHECKED TO KEEP THEM IN GOOD CONDITION.

edges. Wolf teeth sometimes cause discomfort – especially with a bit in the mouth – and may need to be removed by a vet. Poor teeth are often a cause of loss of condition, as food cannot be chewed properly. The tongue can also be cut by sharp edges, which develop as a pony grinds its food. The teeth grow about ¹/₄ cm (¹/₈ in.) a year and are usually worn down at about the same rate. A vet will probably use a rasp to smooth away sharp edges.

Telling the age by the teeth

The front teeth or incisors can be used to tell the age of a pony, a reasonably accurate estimate if the pony is under 12 years old. The milk teeth tend to be small and white, while the permanent teeth are more yellow in colour and so you can estimate the pony's age as the milk teeth are replaced by permanent teeth. The angles of certain teeth, such as the lower incisors, marks such as the galvayne groove (a groove on certain teeth at a certain age) and the length of the teeth can all be examined together in order to estimate the age of an older pony.

Feeding

The subject of feeding is one of the most important parts of caring for your pony. Ponies are natural foragers and have very small stomachs for their size. In the wild they would be eating little and often. The feeding requirements for each pony vary, and many different things can influence this. How much work he is doing, for example, his breed, the time of year, the weather conditions, how much time is spent stabled or out at grass, his size and his temperament.

Ponies cannot be sick and so cannot get rid of anything once swallowed. Eating inappropriate foods or the wrong amounts could cause colic (see page 182), which can be painful for the pony and distressing for you. To simplify things, feed is divided into two main groups, fibre and concentrates. Salt should also be available, in the form of a 'lick', so a pony can help himself to it.

SALT SHOULD BE FREELY AVAILABLE SO THE PONY CAN HAVE IT AS AND WHEN IT NEEDS IT.

Fibre feed

Grass

GRASS IS THE IDEAL PONY FOOD. A WELL-MAINTAINED PASTURE CAN FULFILL MOST NUTRITIONAL NEEDS.

The perfect food for ponies. A pony on good grazing can maintain himself with the simple addition of hay in winter. You need to be careful not to provide too much lush grass in the spring and summer as this can lead to a condition called laminitis (see page 168–69).

Haylage
This is grass that has been harvested, treated and sealed in bags or bales. It is free from dust, which makes it good for ponies that are sensitive to the mould and spores in hay which make them cough and could cause long-term damage. It is more expensive than hay. It is a good idea to use a haylage net, which has much smaller holes in it than a hay net and the food will take longer to get eaten. This is better for the digestion and a stabled pony will have less time to get bored. Buy good-quality haylage and store it outside as long as the packaging stays airtight to protect it from the ingress of water.

FEEDING HAYLAGE IS AN IMPORTANT WAY OF REDUCING THE AMOUNT OF DUST OR MOULD SPORES THAT A SENSITIVE PONY IS EXPOSED TO.

Chaff

Chopped hay or a mix of hay and straw, this can be added to the diet to increase fibre. There are also chaff feeds available, containing alfalfa, which are good for ponies on a high-fibre diet.

HAYLAGE IS GOOD FOR THE DIGESTION.

THIS HAY NET IS POORLY POSITIONED.

Hay

This is made when the grass is cut in the summer and left on the ground to dry out. It is turned a few times and then, after a few days, is baled and stored for feed in the winter. Hay should be made from good-quality pasture and should smell sweet when you pull a handful from the middle of the bale. Meadow hay is cut from a field of permanent pasture that has been allowed to grow long. The quality can vary according to the quality of the pasture. Seed hay is different in that it comes from land that has been re-seeded and therefore contains a variety of good-quality grasses. Seed hay is harder to the touch than meadow hay. There should not be many weeds in the hay and some, such as ragwort, are very poisonous (see page 61). Hay makes the main feed to replace grass in winter or when a pony is stabled. Poor-quality hay is to be avoided at all costs. It is of little nutritional value and the mould and spores can permanently damage a pony's wind, especially if the hay was baled damp. Hay needs to be stored under cover to keep it dry. You need to consider this when deciding how much to buy at a time. Hay is cheaper if you buy it straight from the field, but you cannot use it for six months. Feed hay from a net that is tied at the right height. You can put it on the ground in the field, which is a natural way for a pony to eat it, but there will be some waste. You can also hang it in a net well clear of the ground, but make sure it is not too high or seeds could fall in a pony's eyes when he is eating.

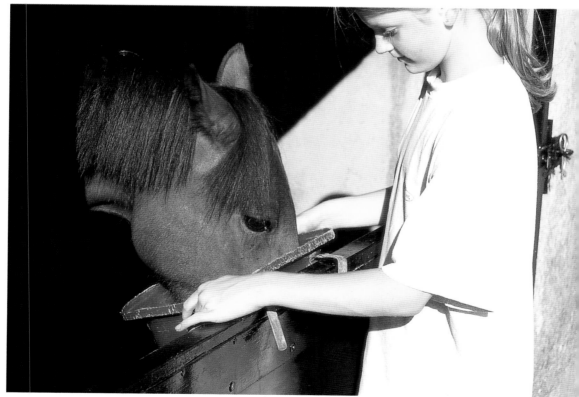

PONIES LOOK FORWARD TO FEEDING TIMES.

CHOP APPLES AND CARROTS TO PREVENT CHOKING.

Silage is best avoided as it can be very high in protein and may cause digestive upsets. Apples and carrots are good, succulent fibre-containing foods. Always chop lengthways to prevent a pony choking.

CHUNKS LIKE THIS CAN BE DANGEROUS.

Concentrates

A native breed of pony doing light hacking may need just grass in the summer with additional hay in the winter. However, those that are stabled or doing harder work will need some concentrates. Cold weather may also have a bearing on this. The simplest way to achieve a balanced diet is to feed a complete feed such as a coarse mix or nuts. This saves you from buying the different ingredients and laboriously mixing them yourself in order to get the balance just right. A variety of mixes and nuts are available to suit most needs, such as low energy nuts, competition mixes, a cool mix (without oats) or a high fibre mix. If you find your pony gets very excitable when you start to feed concentrates, try a low energy mix. Within these mixes are feed stuffs such as oats, barley, maize, molasses, vitamins and minerals. Molasses are a by-product of manufacturing sugar and are very palatable and nutritious to ponies. Chaff can be added to slow down a pony that is bolting his feed. Be careful not to add anything other than carrots and apples or you could upset the balance. Ask your local feed merchant to advise which mix or nut would be appropriate for your pony and always follow the manufacturer's instructions. Remember that the amount needed will be influenced by your pony's energy levels, his current work load, the time of year, the weather, his age, his fitness, breed, condition, and how much grass he is eating. Supplements are not usually necessary, but ask your vet if you think there may be something lacking.

PONY NUTS.

A COARSE MIX.

FEED MIXED TO SUIT THE INDIVIDUAL'S NEEDS.

Golden Rules of Feeding

1. Feed little and often, using the best-quality feeds available.

2. Split any concentrate feed into two or three feeds and spread them throughout the day.

3. Establish a regular daily feeding routine.

4. Provide your pony with a constant supply of fresh, clean water (see below).

5. A constant supply of roughage is essential to keep the digestion moving.

6. Allow an hour's rest between feeding a pony and working it.

7. Each pony's diet must be calculated individually to suit its lifestyle.

8. Keep all your feed buckets and utensils clean.

9. Feed something succulent every day. If your pony has not been at grass, feed the pony some carrots or apples. Remember to cut the carrots lengthways to avoid choking.

10. Do not make any sudden changes to a pony's diet. Introduce new foods gradually, increasing the amounts given over a few days.

STREAMS MAY BE GOOD SOURCES OF WATER, BUT MUST BE ACCESSIBLE AND UNPOLLUTED.

Watering

A clean and constant water supply is essential for maintaining the health and condition of a pony. Without it, your pony will quickly lose condition.

Water in the field

Streams are a good supply of water as long as they have a stony or gravel bottom and not a sandy one – a pony might swallow enough sand to give him colic. A pony must be able to reach the water easily, without having to climb down a bank, for example. Always check that the stream is not polluted further upstream. Also be sure that it runs constantly all year. If it does dry up you will need to find another means. Stagnant ponds are not suitable because water needs to be fresh. They are also dangerous, especially if they have a muddy bottom, and should be fenced off. Automatic troughs are ideal if they are sited away from overhanging trees – which will fill them with leaves – and in a dry, well-drained part of the field, where the ground is less likely to get very muddy in winter. A plug in the bottom makes it easy to empty and scrub out. An automatic trough will probably have a ball cock, which allows the trough to refill as the horse drinks. This must be checked regularly to make sure it is in good working order, especially in the winter when it could be affected by frost. You need to watch for ice in winter, particularly because ponies cannot break it. A plastic ball floating in the water may prevent ice forming.

CHECK AUTOMATIC WATER CONTAINERS REGULARLY.

Water in the stables

An automatic drinking bowl ensures a constant supply of fresh, clean water as long as it is regularly cleaned and inspected. Buckets, again, should have the handles removed or be placed in such a way that a pony cannot get its leg caught easily. Make sure you give two full buckets of water at a time to ensure the pony has enough water overnight. Do not place buckets too close to hay, or they will get clogged up.

HANDLES SHOULD BE REMOVED FROM BUCKETS.

Buckets must have the handles removed and be regularly cleaned and refilled. Remember that ponies drink up to 8 to 10 gallons of water per day, so make sure you provide enough buckets full for the number of ponies in the field. Other containers can be used, but should not have any sharp edges, which can cause injuries.

Handling your pony

Ponies will usually move away from pressure. In order to ask your pony to move over, place a hand on his side and apply a little pressure. Use the same words each time such as 'move over' and he will soon learn what is expected.

You need to be able to lift all of the pony's legs for grooming and for checking the feet. To lift a front leg, face the tail, remembering always to talk to your pony. Starting at the shoulder, run your hand down his leg and tendons to the fetlock joint then put a little upward pressure on the joint and say 'up'. Don't lift the foot too high as this will be uncomfortable for the pony. If he does not pick up his foot straight away, lean on his shoulder a little, which will encourage him to shift the weight to the other leg. To lift a hind leg, stand by the pony's hip facing the tail. Start at the pony's bottom and run your hand down the back of the leg until you reach the hock. Then move your hand round to the front of the leg and down to the fetlock joint. Again, apply a little upward pressure and say 'up'. When you want to put the foot down lower it gently to the floor, never drop it.

One of the areas of handling which is often carried out incorrectly, and which can result in an accident, is turning a pony out in the field. Open the gate wide enough, and make sure that it does not start to close on you and your pony as you walk through. Push the gate open and walk through. Turn the pony away from you in a circle, stand facing the gate, and close it. Never release a pony straight into the field as he may canter off, kicking up his heels as he goes and kicking you in the process. In all aspects of handling a pony you must be patient and well mannered, making everything you do with him a pleasure and safe. Always give him clear instructions and treat him with kindness. You will soon build up mutual respect.

Catching your pony

Whenever you go to catch your pony, whether it is out in the field or in the stable, you must always approach quietly and confidently. He must be aware that you are approaching so that you don't startle him. Always approach by walking up to a pony's shoulder – he cannot see you if you approach from behind – and be careful not to make any sudden or loud noises. Remember that, in the wild, ponies are flight animals, escaping from predators or dangerous situations by running away. It is of the utmost importance to talk to your pony before and during handling him, and your voice will soon become familiar to him. Pat or stroke him on his lower neck or shoulder and slip the rope around his neck quietly. Place the noseband over his muzzle and then put the headpiece quietly behind his ears. Do up the buckle, and pat the pony again. Never try to lead a pony with just a rope around his neck, or lean over a gate from the wrong side to put on the head collar. If you want to reward your pony for being caught easily, take a piece of apple or carrot with you. It is not a good idea to do this every time, however, as he will soon learn to expect it.

Some ponies can be awkward to catch, usually when you only have a limited amount of time. In such cases you must be patient and keep your cool. Never try to grab the pony or corner him – he is much bigger and stronger than you – and never lose your temper. Never scold him for being awkward. You can try leaving a head collar on in the field but make sure its well fitting. Generally, it is not a good idea to leave them on in case the pony gets caught up in something or gets a leg in it when rolling or scratching. You could also try leaving a short length of rope attached to it, to give you something to get hold of. You could try walking around him in large circles, or walking away from him. Ponies can be very curious to know what you are up to. Some ponies will suddenly become a lot easier to catch if they know you have food, but this could mean having to remove any other ponies from the field first. Never take a bucket of food into a field full of ponies or you will cause a fight and may get stuck in the middle of it. If you begin to lose your temper, go away and come back later. Make sure that your pony always thinks of you coming to the field as something to look forward to. It will earn your pony's respect if you are confident and firm, but always treat him with kindness.

ALWAYS TALK TO YOUR PONY WHILE APPROACHING BEFORE CATCHING HIM.

USE A PROPER HEADCOLLAR AND ROPE TO CATCH YOUR PONY IN THE FIELD.

A PONY COULD GET A LEG CAUGHT IN THIS DANGLING HEAD COLLAR – ALWAYS TIDY UP YOUR EQUIPMENT.

Leading your pony

To be safe and to avoid your pony taking you for a walk or treading on your feet, you must learn how to lead him correctly. Always use a proper lead rope rather than a cord or string, which can hurt your hands. It is advisable to wear gloves, and you should never wrap the lead rope around your hand. If your pony is startled and takes off you could end up being dragged. A pony is usually led from the left or near side, but should accept being led from either. To lead a pony in a head collar, hold the rope in your right hand about 30 cm (12 in.) from his chin. Hold the other end of the rope in your left hand, making sure you keep the end well off the ground. Walk beside the pony's head or shoulder and do not get left behind or try to pull him along from in front. To turn him, always push him gently away from you so that you avoid getting trodden on. Do not hold him by the head collar or on too short a rope, as this will make him feel uncomfortable. Too long a rope, however, would mean that you have much less control if the pony makes a sudden movement. If you are leading a pony while it is tacked up, take the reins over his head and lead as before. Do not lead a pony with a very loose girth or with dangling stirrups. If you are leading on the road, it is safer to wear your hat,

ALWAYS USE A HEADCOLLAR AND ROPE TO LEAD YOUR PONY.

and lead in a bridle as you will have more control. Walk between the pony and the on-coming traffic. Lightly coloured or fluorescent clothing will make you more visible to motorists.

Tying up your pony

Tying up your pony safely is essential. Many accidents occur when ponies are not tied up correctly or are tied to unsuitable objects. Even a pony that is normally very quiet can be startled by something, and it is important that you know how to tie a quick-release knot.

If you are tying your pony to a metal ring on a wall, attach a loop of breakable cord to the ring first and then tie the lead rope to that. The cord should be strong enough not to break with the normal movement of the pony's head, but weak enough to break if the pony was to pull back suddenly.

WALK BESIDE THE PONY: DO NOT PULL HIM FROM THE FRONT OR ALLOW HIM TO DRAG YOU BEHIND.

ATTACH A LOOP OF BREAKABLE STRING TO THE WALL RING, THEN TIE THE LEAD ROPE TO IT.

ALWAYS TIE YOUR PONY SAFELY — A FRIGHTENED HORSE COULD LIFT THIS GATE OFF ITS HINGES WITH DISASTROUS EFFECT.

Dos and Don'ts:

Never leave your pony alone while tied up in case he gets into trouble.

Never leave him tied too close to anything that he could get entangled in or kick at.

Never tie up close to other ponies in case they start a fight.

Never tie up to a movable object, such as a trash can or a gate.

Always use a quick release knot which allows you to free a pony quickly if he gets into trouble.

Always use a proper head collar and lead rope and do not tie a pony up by its bridle.

Don't tie up too short as a pony will panic if he cannot move his head.

Don't tie up too long as a pony could get caught up in the slack rope.

WITH BASIC CARE, MAINTENANCE AND ATTENTION, YOUR PONY WILL BE CONTENT AND COMFORTABLE.

Pony Health

Pony Health

It is important that you learn to tell when a pony is unwell, and once you get to know your pony this will become easier. A knowledgeable person may be able to help you deal with minor problems, but in some cases, or if you are unsure, it is best to call a vet. Some conditions can cause a pony to deteriorate very quickly so it is advisable to get veterinary help as soon as you notice something is wrong. It is better to be safe than sorry, and calling a vet could prevent serious problems before they really get started.

Your pony should have a shiny coat and supple skin in summer. A stable-kept pony will be shiny in winter too. A pony's eyes should be bright and alert with the membranes under the eyelid moist and a salmon-pink colour. A pony's ears should flick back and forth, and he should look interested in his surroundings. He should be neither too fat nor too thin, but well covered. You should be able to feel the ribs underneath the skin, but you should not be able to see them. A pony's legs and feet should be cool to the touch, with no patches of heat or swelling. He should drink regularly and have a good appetite – loss of interest in food is a sign that

CORRECT CARE AND FEEDING WILL SHOW IN A SHINY, SUPPLE COAT. THIS HORSE IS STILL LOOKING BRIGHT AND WELL AT OVER 20 YEARS OLD.

CHECK THAT YOUR PONY HAS EATEN ALL HIS FEED.

something is wrong. A pony's weight should be evenly spread on all four legs and he should not be lame, when he walks. Resting a hind leg is normal. Urine should be passed regularly without effort and should be a pale yellow colour or clear. Droppings will vary according to diet, but they should not be too runny. There should not be any discharge from the nostrils or any coughing. Pony's breathe approximately eight to 12 times per minute. This is easier to see when a pony is resting – stand towards the back of him and watch his side moving in and out. You may need to take your pony's temperature. The thermometer should be shaken until it reaches 37.4°C or (100°F). It should be well greased and inserted under the tail into the rectum, get an experienced person to do this. Hold firmly in place for about 30 seconds. The normal temperature for a pony is

38°c (100.5°F). If it is over 1 degree more or less you should call the vet. Pulse rate should be between 36 and 42 beats per minute when the pony is resting. To take a pony's pulse find the artery under his jaw, behind his eye or on the inside of the foreleg, level with the knee where the artery goes over the bone. Press two fingers lightly to feel the pulse. It is wise to keep a note of your pony's normal temperature, pulse rate and breathing rate at rest and compare them with readings you take when you think you pony is unwell. Unless it is a very hot day, your pony should not sweat when resting.

If your pony sustains a serious injury, phone the vet immediately. If your pony has a problem with its feet seek advice from your farrier. Do not ride your pony if you think it is unwell.

EXERCISE IS ESSENTIAL TO ENSURE GOOD CONDITION.

'Condition' is the term used for the amount of flesh your pony is carrying, basically whether the pony is too fat, too thin or just right. To maintain a good condition a pony must have balanced feed and exercise. Too much feed with not enough exercise will cause a pony to become fat, possibly leading to such problems as laminitis, heart strain and lameness. Not enough feed and a lot of exercise will produce a thin pony. As your experience grows you will learn to maintain good condition by adjusting your pony's diet and management. Until then, seek advice from an expert or a vet if your pony is losing condition.

THIS PONY NEEDS A LITTLE LESS FOOD AND MORE EXERCISE.

Causes of poor condition

- The pony does not have a fresh, clean constant water supply.

- Nutrition is vitally important.

- Your pony may be intimidated by other ponies at feeding time.

- Your pony may lack certain minerals.

- Older ponies find it less easy to keep weight on as a rule, and when over about 16 years, need to be kept warm in winter and may be harder to maintain in condition.

- Sharp teeth may be causing eating difficulties.

- A pony may be suffering from worms.

- A pony may be suffering from disease.

- Ponies kept alone and confined to the stable for long periods may develop compulsive habits and lossof condition.

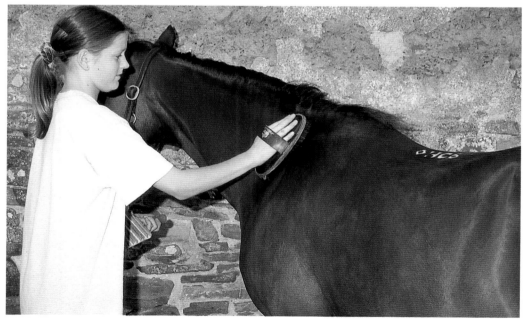

KEEP GROOMING TO A MINIMUM IF YOUR PONY IS SICK.

Common conditions and ailments

Do not be alarmed by this section. Although accidents and illnesses are sometimes difficult to prevent, good stable management and proper care should help reduce the risk of some of them. A pony that is unwell or injured will need to be kept warm and comfortable. If kept in the stable, he will need a thick comfortable bed, plenty of fresh air, regular attention and, ideally, a companion nearby. Each pony will need individual nursing depending on the condition or injury and his normal lifestyle. Here are some general hints on nursing a sick pony. Grooming need only be enough to ensure he is kept comfortable. He must be kept warm. Take advice from your vet on what to feed him but as a general rule feed him little and often. If he doesn't eat, take the food away. Do not leave it in the stable, but offer fresh feed a little later. Try to add a chopped or grated apple or carrot to encourage him to eat. Fresh, clean water must be available at all times, as well as a salt lick. If he is confined to the stable he will appreciate a few handfuls of fresh grass (never feed cut grass or lawn clippings, as these could cause a tummy ache). Do not leave the grass in the stable if he doesn't eat it.

If your pony has a temperature it is essential to keep him warm with light rugs. A sweat rug (see page 35) under a light rug will trap a layer of warm air, which will help if he is sweating. Keep the stable well ventilated but without draughts. Stable bandages (see page 90), will help keep his legs warm if needed. If your pony has something contagious and needs to be kept in isolation, move him to a stable well away from the others and use separate equipment for mucking out and grooming. Do not go near other ponies while you are looking after him, as you risk spreading the disease yourself. Exercise and turning out in the field should be reintroduced gradually if a pony has had a spell of being confined.

Pests

FLIES CAN IRRITATE A PONIES SENSITIVE EYES AND IN THESE CASES A FLY MASK IS USEFUL.

Worms

All ponies carry some worms in their gut, which vary in size from thin threads to the thickness of a pencil and several inches long. Most of them lay eggs in large number in the pony's intestines, having been picked up by the pony while grazing. Good pasture management and regular treatment with a wormer every six to eight weeks helps keep the numbers of worms down. A pony with an excessive amount of worms will have a dull coat, will lose weight and may have a potbelly.

You can treat a pony with worms by putting powder in its feed or by using a syringe to squirt medication down the pony's throat. Be careful to give the correct dose and to follow the manufacturer's instructions. Some preparations don't cover all types of worm so always read the label carefully. If you are unsure, take advice from your vet. If more than one pony shares a field, then all of them must be treated at the same time or the worms will continue to spread between them.

Picking up droppings regularly will help prevent so many worms getting into the pasture. It is best to keep the pony off the pasture for a minimum of 48 hours after worming so as not to re-infect the pasture. If this is not possible, pick up droppings as often as possible over the few days after the treatment.

FEED SOMETHING SUCCULENT DAILY.

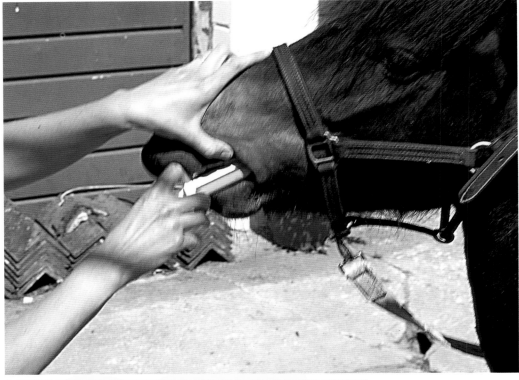

A SYRINGE IS THE QUICKEST AND EASIEST METHOD OF ADMINISTERING A WORMER.

Lice

These are small pale brown insects. Some types of lice bite, while others suck blood. The blood-sucking lice are normally found in the mane and tail areas and the biting variety are more often found on the legs. Ponies that have been neglected can be badly affected by lice and they will be spread all over the body and head areas. On close examination the lice can be seen amongst the scurf or on the pony's hairs.

Lice are less easy to see on a pony at grass with a thick winter coat, so you will need to be more watchful. Ponies rub and scratch the affected areas and this can lead to unsightly bald patches. Seek advice from your vet about how to treat this irritating parasite.

Mange

This is a condition caused by mites that bite. They live on or burrow into the skin causing severe itching. The hair becomes thin, leaving bald patches with scabs and the skin thickens. Mange is easily spread from one pony to another through close contact, even a shared grooming kit, but is more often seen in ponies that are not very well looked after. Seek advice and treatment from your vet. The stable and all your equipment will need to be disinfected,with all bedding burned to eliminate the pest completely.

Warbles

Warble flies look like small bees and usually lay their eggs on cattle; they are more commonly found on ponies that share a field with cattle. The larvae hatch after a few days then burrow into the skin. In the spring the grubs accumulate under the skin on the animal's back, where they form a small bump or swelling. They often cause a problem if the swelling is underneath the saddle area. Applying a poultice may encourage the maggots to appear, in which case they can be brushed off. Do not squeeze the swelling as this could lead to a nasty

STABLE RUGS PROTECT PONIES AND HORSES FROM DRAUGHTS AND CHILLS IN STABLES.

abscess. In the early summer the full-grown grub emerges and falls to the ground to pupate. After about three weeks a warble fly emerges. Seek advice from your vet if your pony is infected with a warble. It is not advisable to ride a pony with any type of sore underneath the saddle.

WARBLE FLIES FROM CATTLE MAY INFECT PONIES.

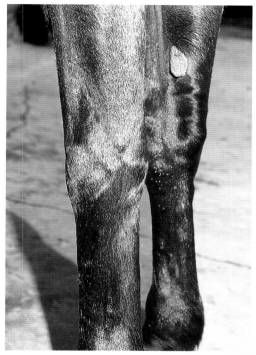

BOT EGGS MUST BE REMOVED TO AVOID INGESTION.

Bots

Bot eggs are little yellow eggs that attach to the hairs of a pony's legs in summer, and ponies often swallow them as they lick their legs. The grubs attach themselves to the inside of the stomach and feed off the pony until late spring. They are potentially very dangerous and can be fatal. A wormer can rid a pony of bots in the stomach, usually carried out in the autumn, and the yellow eggs can be scraped off a pony's legs with a special knife.

Ticks

Ticks are common and can be found on most domestic animals. They usually attach themselves to a horse's head during grazing and can grow to about 1 cm (½ in.) before they drop off. You should never pull a tick off, as part of its body usually remains in the skin and can cause infection. Seek advice from the vet on how to treat a pony with ticks.

Lameness

At some time or another, your pony is likely to go lame. This is quite common and can result from a variety of causes, either by injury or disease. In all cases you must consult your vet for diagnosis and treatment. Lameness could affect any part of the leg, its joints or the foot. Never ride a pony that is lame. If you are out on a hack when he goes lame dismount, and check that there is not simply a stone in his shoe. If not, lead him home quietly. Rest is of great importance when treating lameness, as is a comfortable stable. If a pony is lame on one foreleg the other foreleg may need to be supported with a bandage to ease the extra strain on it.

It is important that you are able to tell when a pony is lame, and helpful if you can tell which

leg is causing the trouble. This is not always as easy as it sounds. Severe lameness will be obvious at a walk. If it is not, get someone to trot the pony on a loose rein towards and away from you in a straight line and on hard ground. If the pony is lame on a foreleg he will lower or dip his head when the good leg comes to the ground. If lame in both front legs he will hold his head up and take short strides. If lame in a hind leg his quarters will dip more as the good leg comes to the ground, as the pony tries to keep the weight of the painful leg. When standing still one leg may be rested or one foreleg may be pointed forwards. Common causes of lameness are noted below.

Laminitis

Found more often in ponies than in horses, laminitis is a very painful condition caused by inflammation of the tissues inside the hoof. Because the hoof is enclosed in a solid case that cannot expand, the inflammation causes a pony great pain. Reasons for the swelling might be an inappropriate amount of feed or too much lush green grass. It can also be brought on by a fever and inflammation of the womb in mares. Too much lush grass is the most common cause in ponies, along with too much hard work on a hard surface. Wild ponies are used to managing on moorland, which is sparse with poor-quality grazing. They need to

TROT YOUR PONY ALONG HARD AND LEVEL GROUND TO ASSESS WHICH LEG IS LAME.

walk a long way to find adequate food. A pony on good pasture will soon have eaten more than he needs to maintain himself, even if he is working, but will tend to carry on eating. This will lead to the pony developing a form of indigestion that poisons the blood stream, in turn resulting in the inflammation of the sensitive tissue in the hoof.

A pony with laminitis will stand with his front feet pushed forwards and his hind feet underneath him so as to take the pressure and

YOUR FARRIER SHOULD BE ABLE TO ADVISE YOU ON FOOT PROBLEMS

weight off the toes. The foot will change shape and he will be unwilling to move. The hooves feel warm or hot to the touch and, although the symptoms are more commonly seen in the front feet, all four can be affected. A temperature of up to 41°C (104°F) will probably be present and the pony will obviously be in pain. Veterinary advice should be sought immediately, and painkillers may be given if acute pain is obvious. In the meantime, the pony should be stabled with a nice thick bed to encourage him to lie down. Shavings are best because they help to support the soles of the feet. A farrier will offer advice on footcare, possibly fitting special shoes.

The risk of laminitis can be greatly reduced if you keep your pony off very lush grass. However, some ponies are more prone than others to laminitis and they need to be monitored carefully, particularly in the spring and summer. Poorer quality grazing is often better for these ponies and it may help to stable them for a given time each day, or to use an electric fence to regulate the amount of grazing they have access to each day. You can prevent a laminitis-prone pony from suffering a second time by maintaining a delicate balance between nutrition and exercise.

Mud fever

This condition is most often found in ponies kept at grass in the winter, when conditions are wet and muddy. Not all ponies are affected, and the type of soil may be a factor too. Clay soil is particularly irritating. The thin skin around the heels becomes irritated and inflamed, making the heel become sore and cracked. Bacteria are then able to get into the skin resulting in a temperature and lameness. The skin will continue to crack unless a soothing, moist ointment is applied throughout the healing process. Try using a thin layer of petroleum jelly on the heels and pasterns if the skin is becoming inflamed, and do not wash a pony's legs in winter, unless they are exceptionally dry, as leaving them damp in cold conditions contributes to this problem. If a stabled pony comes back from a ride with wet and muddy legs, cover them with stable bandages for a few hours until dry and then remove the bandages and brush off the mud with a soft brush. In very muddy conditions, this condition can also affect the under-belly area.

Sprains

These can occur in the muscles, tendons or ligaments. They can be caused during jumping or riding fast in heavy soil, particularly when the pony is tired or unfit. Obvious signs of a sprain are heat and /or swelling in the limbs. Run cold water over the swelling until the vet arrives. This will make the pony more comfortable and will help to reduce the heat and swelling. Tendon and ligament strains are more common in the front legs than in the hind.

Curb

A curb is when the ligament in the hind leg, where the point of the hock meets the top of the cannon bone, becomes strained. It appears to thicken and bulge. When it is forming, it will feel warm to touch and may cause lameness.

Soft swellings

Also known as bursal enlargements, these are caused by injuries or strains to the joints, tendons or ligaments. They have various names depending on where they are situated. If you detect any of the following, contact your vet and do not ride your pony in the meantime. Run a cold hose over the affected area to reduce heat and swelling.

A bog spavin is a soft swelling around the inside and to the front of the hock. A wind gall is a soft swelling just above and at the sides of the fetlock. It doesn't usually cause lameness

once established, although the swelling often remains. Capped elbow – swelling at the elbow – is often caused when lying down without enough bedding. Capped hock – swelling on the hock – can be caused by lack of bedding or, sometimes, while travelling without enough protection from boots. Thoroughpin is a soft swelling in the dip just in front of the point of the hock.

Bony enlargements

These are bony lumps that form in various parts of the leg, most often the result of concussion. They often cause lameness when they are forming but, once formed, do not cause further problems. Bony enlargements are most likely to occur in young ponies, especially if they do a lot of work on a hard surface. Heat is often present in the affected area. Veterinary attention will be needed. Ring bone is a bony enlargement on the pastern. Side bones are bony enlargements near the heel. They appear as a hard ridge where the cartilage has gradually changed to form bony lumps. A bone spavin is a bony enlargement on the inside of the hock, which needs to be treated promptly and can cause lameness for quite a while. Splints are bony enlargements on the splint or cannon bone, usually on the inside of the

RUNNING COLD WATER OVER A SPRAIN CAN EASE IT AND REDUCE SWELLING.

SEEDY TOE IS PARTICULARLY COMMON IN DONKEYS.

foreleg. Less commonly, they can be found on the hind legs or on the outside of the foreleg. In many cases they have formed by the time the pony is aged seven.

Bruised sole

This is quite common when the pony has had a stone lodged in his shoe, which has caused a bruise to the sensitive sole of the foot. Some ponies are more prone to this than others, especially those ridden on stony ground. If it keeps happening, it is possible to fit a leather pad under the shoe to protect the sole.

Navicular disease

This is caused when the navicular bone in the foot becomes pitted and rough. Pain results as the tendon runs across the bone. A pony with navicular disease will often stand with one leg pointed forwards. Corrective shoeing may help, but this is a serious condition.

Thrush

This is a smelly condition that affects the frog (the V-shaped part of the sole). It can often result from poor stable management, for example when a pony has been standing in wet muck or if the feet are not picked out regularly. You should consult your vet or farrier if your pony's feet smell.

Cracks

These can appear in the wall of the hoof with a variety of causes. A sand crack starts at the coronet band at the top of the hoof and heads downwards, often on the hind foot near the toe. A similar crack nearer to the heel is called a quarter crack. They can be painful and need attention.

Broken hoof walls

Pieces of hoof can actually break off in chunks when a pony loses a shoe. An unshod pony may get bits breaking off through wear and tear. A farrier will tidy these up.

Gravel

This is the name given to describe when a small object such as a piece of grit or gravel has been pushed up into the hoof, causing pain and pressure under the hoof wall. Pain will be felt when the hoof wall is tapped and an abscess may form under the hoof wall. If left untreated, it could travel upwards and eventually break out at the coronet band.

Seedy toe

This condition can be caused by poor shoeing, especially where the toe clip is too tight. It can also be caused by an injury to the foot. A hollow forms near the toe, which is actually the separation of the hoof wall from the fleshy tissue underneath. The hollow then becomes filled with a dry crumbly horn. It is common in donkeys and needs attention from the farrier.

Pricked foot

This is caused when the farrier drives a nail into the sensitive part of the foot by mistake while shoeing. It is an accident that occurs from time to time and does not cause too much trouble unless it becomes infected, when it should be treated as a puncture wound.

Punctured sole

This is when a foreign body such as a nail or a sharp stone punctures the sole of the foot. The wound tends to heal over quickly, leaving dirt and bacteria inside, which then leads to infection or an abscess. This is very painful as it

creates pressure inside the foot. A hole will need to be made to allow the abscess to drain and a poultice will need to be applied. Antibiotics may also be needed. Check that your own tetanus vaccination is up to date.

Corns

These are bruises that form in the sole, behind the heel on either side of the frog. The sole is quite thin and sensitive here. Corns can be caused by pressure from a shoe. Attention from the farrier is needed, who may cut it out. The wound then needs to be kept clean to prevent an abscess forming. Special shoes can be fitted to ponies that are prone to corns. They transfer the weight to another part of the hoof. Future shoeing must ensure there is no pressure on that part of the sole.

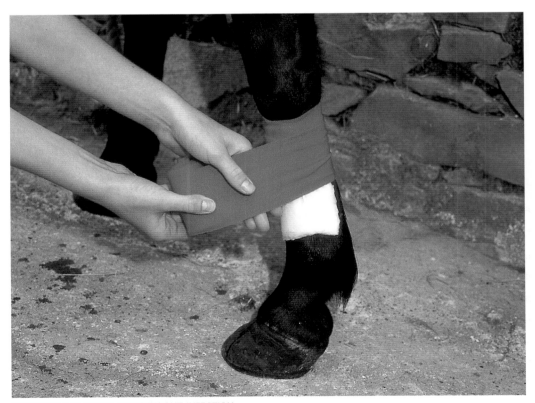

POULTICES ARE USEFUL TO DRAW OUT INFECTION.

Skin conditions

Sweet itch

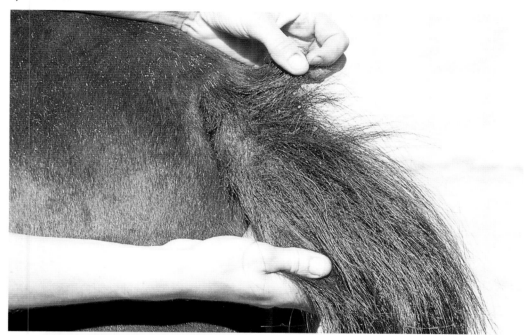

A PONY WILL SOON MESS AND TANGLE ITS MANE OR TAIL IF THEY ITCH IT A GREAT DEAL.

Some ponies are particularly sensitive to irritating bites from midges and can rub themselves bald. This usually happens near the mane and anywhere on a line from the poll, (behind the ears) to the top of the tail. This condition is thought to be due to an allergic reaction to midge saliva. A pony with sweet itch will quickly rub out its mane and tail making it sore, difficult to plait and unsightly. A vet can give you a lotion that can be applied to soothe the irritation. Ponies are usually affected from late spring to early autumn, the worst times being a couple of hours before sunset and a couple of hours after sunrise, and they are best brought in at these times. Prevention, by managing the time spent outside and applying lotion twice a day, will help maintain the mane and tail in the summer.

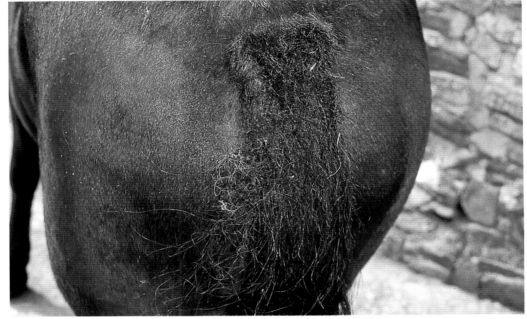

A GOOD TAIL CAN QUICKLY BE RUINED BY SWEET ITCH.

Galls and sores

Most often caused by saddles or rugs that do not fit properly or that have sweat and grease underneath, galls and sores are patches of red, sore and inflamed skin that often appear on the withers or around the girth area. Areas that have been damaged in the past show as white patches where the skin has been damaged. Galls are patches of red, sore and inflamed skin. An anaesthetic powder or cream can be applied to soothe the skin until it is completely healed. If an ill-fitting saddle is the cause of a gall or sore, get the fit checked. The same applies to rugs. A piece of sheepskin can be sewn into the withers area of a rug to prevent rubbing. Vests are also available that help stop the rug rubbing against the shoulders. Girths can also be covered with a sleeve of furry material. Young ponies and those which have not been ridden for a while will gall more easily because their skin is more tender.

Rain scold

Caused by spells of heavy rain, this condition is

unlikely to occur if your pony is well cared for with adequate shelter and rugs, particularly in the winter. The hair falls out and the skin becomes sore and is susceptible to infection. Seek advice from the vet for treatment, and provide better protection from the weather.

Ringworm

Ringworm is a very infectious skin condition, caused by a fungus and showing itself as bald, circular patches about 5 cm (2 in.) in diameter.

It is easily spread between ponies in a yard, particularly with shared grooming or tack. It does not appear to itch but can be very unsightly resulting in large bald patches. If your vet confirms ringworm, it is best to isolate a pony if possible and keep all equipment separate. Disinfect everything before using on another pony and wash your hands before you touch other animals and people – humans can catch this too. Rubber gloves are recommended when dealing with a pony with ringworm.

LOTIONS ARE AVAILABLE FROM VETS TO TREAT SWEET ITCH. ALWAYS WEAR GLOVE WHEN APPLYING IT.

Respiratory problems

YOUR VET WILL BE ABLE TO ASSESS ANY RESPIRATORY PROBLEMS.

Broken wind

Several things can cause broken wind, including galloping a pony which is unfit or that has recently had a feed, and constant exposure to the dust and mould found in hay and straw. It may also be the result of pneumonia. Broken wind is a condition of the lungs that causes a a double breathing action on exhalation. The pony develops a deep cough and is no longer capable of doing any fast work.

Chronic Obstructive Pulmonary Disease (COPD)

Dust and mould in hay and straw affects some ponies by irritating the lungs and causing the small air tubes in the lungs to get blocked with discharge. If this is left unattended, the lungs eventually become so damaged that the pony has to force itself to breath to get enough oxygen It does this by using muscles that it wouldn't normally use, resulting in a double breath on exhalation. This can eventually lead to broken wind (see above). Good management can reduce the number of mould spores. Use an alternative type of bedding, such as shavings and feeding haylage (see page 39) or hay soaked in water for 30 minutes and drained. Ponies affected by this condition will thrive better out in fresh air as long as adequate food and shelter are provided. If they do need to be stabled, ensure good ventilation. Note that it is normal for a pony to cough a couple of times occasionally if followed by a brisk blow through the nostrils.

Roaring and whistling

More common in horses than ponies, this is a condition of the larynx where airflow is restricted, causing the horse to make rasping noises as it breathes when cantering or galloping. The noise is made when a paralysed vocal cord that has become loose in the larynx partly blocks the air passage. Horses with this condition can become short of breath when doing fast work. The condition will not improve on its own, and you must seek advice from a vet.

Pneumonia

Pneumonia is inflammation of the lungs. Causes include an infection, virus and fungi. Symptoms are a high temperature, fast breathing and a cough. Discharge can be coughed up from the lungs. A pony with pneumonia must be rested and carefully nursed. Call the vet immediately. Return to work after this condition should be very gradual as the lungs can take a long time to recover.

Coughs

It is not unusual for a horse to cough, for example if a particle of food becomes stuck, or when he clears his throat when first taken out to exercise, usually followed by a good blow through the nostrils. However, a cough may sometimes be caused by pneumonia (see above) or some other inflammation of the lungs such as COPD (see above), influenza (see page 182), a virus or a cold. In all instances, veterinary advice and treatment should be sought immediately. A cough needs to be investigated, even if the pony seems otherwise well, in order to minimise the risk of permanent damage.

Diseases

Strangles

A very contagious disease, strangles will rapidly spread through an entire yard if infected ponies are not isolated. It can occur at any age but young ponies are particularly vulnerable. Ponies with strangles develop a high temperature and have a thick discharge from the nostrils. Abscesses develop around the throat and under the jaw that cause distress and discomfort when

the pony tries to swallow. After about ten days the abscesses burst and discharge pus. This gives a pony some instant relief after which he will gradually return to good health. Bastard strangles is a variant of this condition, when the infection spreads through the blood stream causing abscesses to form in other parts of the body, sometimes the lungs. This is much more dangerous to a pony, and he should be isolated immediately. Treatment will involve eating food that is easy to swallow, a good deal of rest and, sometimes, holding a warm cloth on an abscess to encourage it to ripen, thus speeding recovery. This should not be carried out without the advice of a vet, however.

Tetanus

Easily avoided by vaccination and very difficult to cure, tetanus is extremely serious and can be fatal. A germ that lives in the soil and thrives in droppings, tetanus gets into a pony's body usually via a wound. About ten days later the pony will develop a high temperature and stiffness, and the membranes of the eye will partly cover the eyeball. Later the jaw seizes up making feeding difficult. Keep the pony quiet and call the vet immediately.

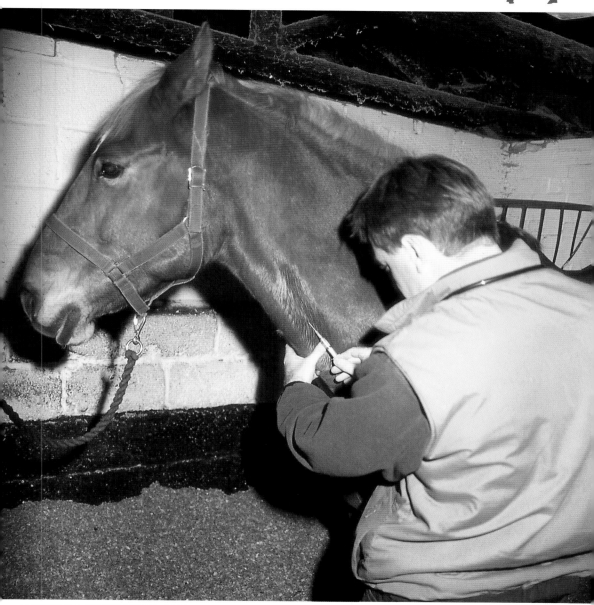

TETANUS IS A SERIOUS AILMENT WHICH IS EASILY PREVENTED BY VACCINATION.

Equine influenza

Another complaint that can be largely prevented by vaccination, equine influenza is very contagious and cases must be isolated as soon as possible. It is a virus which shows itself as a high temperature and a general sense of being unwell, There will be a loss of appetite, a cough and discharge from the nostrils. The membranes of the eyes and gums become inflamed and tears fall down the face. The breathing rate is increased due to the inflammation in the lungs. Recovery usually takes about 14 days, but great care should be taken to reintroduce the pony to work gradually because of the damage to the heart and lungs. Veterinary attention and careful nursing will be required.

Dietary problems

Colic

Colic is generally described as tummy ache and can vary from a mild pain to a fatal twisted gut. Most of the causes are to do with the diet – grass clippings that have heated up, for example. Hay that has not been stored for long enough before use or is mouldy can cause colic, as can too much hard feed immediately before or after work. Other causes may be when ponies eat their food too quickly, a bout of worms, giving a large quantity of cold water to a hot and tired pony, or eating poisonous plants.

There are various symptoms. A pony will turn to look at his flanks or will begin to kick his belly. He may roll or throw himself on the floor. Heart rate is increased and there is obvious pain. The belly may look bloated. A complication of colic is when the pony throws himself down and rolls, while also suffering from trapped wind and muscle spasms. This can cause the bowel to twist which is often fatal. If your pony gets colic you need to call the vet. The pony will need a deep comfortable bed, and leading him around can help to stop him throwing himself down. Try to keep him warm. If he is sweating put a sweat rug underneath a lighter rug to trap a layer of warm air and so helping to keep him warm and dry (see page 35). Colic might pass within a couple of hours, while other bouts can take much longer. Do not feed a pony during an attack and give the pony water in small amounts when he is quieter. To help prevent colic ensure good stable management and follow the rules of feeding together with a regular worming programme.

Poisoning

Immediate veterinary help is essential if you suspect your pony may have been poisoned. Causes can include weed killer, rat poison, overdose of medicine, poisonous plants (see page 61), mouldy feed and polluted water. A huge variety of symptoms can be the result of poisoning, depending on the cause, and can include colic, diarrhoea, loss of appetite, weakness, staggering, collapse, trembling and an increased heart rate. As a pony cannot be sick, he will digest and absorb any poison that he has swallowed.

Wounds

A wound could be in the form of a bruise, puncture wound, clean cut or tear.

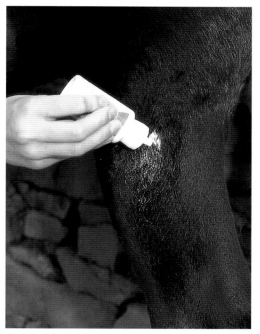

APPLY WOUND POWDER TO PREVENT INFECTION.

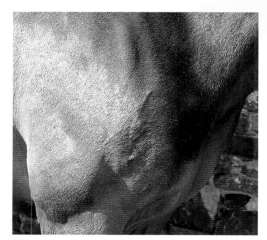

LARGE CUTS OFTEN LEAVE A SCAR.

Clean cut and tear wounds

Anything sharp can cut the skin. If bleeding occurs, place a clean cloth over it and apply a little pressure until it stops. The wound needs to be properly cleaned and any dirt, grit or other foreign bodies must be removed. You can do this either by putting a poultice on or hosing the area with cold water, then carefully wiping away any dirt and grit with a clean cloth. If you cannot stop the bleeding, bandage over the clean cloth to keep it in place and call the vet.

Poultices

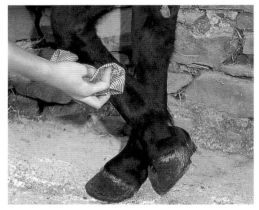

1 Wash and clean the wound thoroughly to remove dirt and foreign bodies.

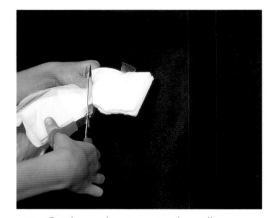

2 Cut the poultice to a size that will generously cover and overlap the wound.

5 Secure the bandage by tying the tapes. Be careful not to tie them too tight or directly over the wound itself.

3 Soak the poultice in hot water and allow to cool to body temperature before applying.

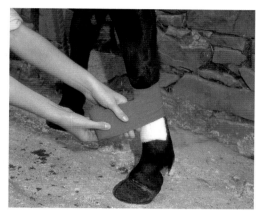

4 Position the poultice over the wound and hold in place with a bandage.

To test the temperature of a poultice, place it on your elbow and it should feel comfortable. Cut it to the correct size and place it sticky-side-down on the wound. Always follow the manufacturer's instructions. When cooled and held in place with a bandage, the poultice will help to draw out any impurities and will reduce the inflammation. Once clean (if a poultice is not needed), the wound can be sprayed with an antiseptic spray or squirted with wound powder. Call a vet if you think the wound may need stitching. Antibiotics may be needed in some cases, and you should check that the pony's tetanus is up to date. Small scrapes are often best left uncovered and will soon heal.

Bandages

1 Before rolling, fold the bandage so the tapes are on the inside.

2 Using your leg for support, roll up the whole bandage firmly.

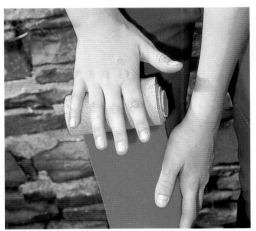

3 Once rolled, secure the bandage with an elastic band to keep it secure.

Keeping the bandages clean and rolled up correctly is very useful if you need them in a hurry.

Puncture wounds

These happen when a nail or other sharp object pierces a pony, usually in the foot, leaving a small but deep wound with a very small entrance site. The wound soon heals over, often leaving dirt and grime behind, and this can cause an infection or abscess. This type of wound often goes unnoticed until the growing infection causes pain. A farrier or vet will locate the point of entry, and will probably open up the wound to allow it to drain. Use the poultice as you would for a clean cut, to draw out the infection. Cover the foot with a poultice, boot or bandage and change the dressing twice daily. When the pony is sound continue for a further 48 hours to ensure that the infection does not flare up again. Antibiotics may be needed and you should check that the pony's tetanus is up to date. The outside of the wound needs to be kept open until the inside is properly healed.

Bruises

Knocks causing bruising can result from a fall, inadequate bandaging while travelling, kicks from another pony, or from a pony brushing and treading on himself. They do not always break the skin but will cause bleeding, swelling and inflammation under the skin. Running a cold hose over the injury will help reduce the swelling and discomfort during the first 24 hours. After that, applying a warm poultice will soothe it and reduce inflammation. These types of wounds are painful even if the skin is not broken.

RUN A COLD HOSE OVER A SWOLLEN BRUISE.

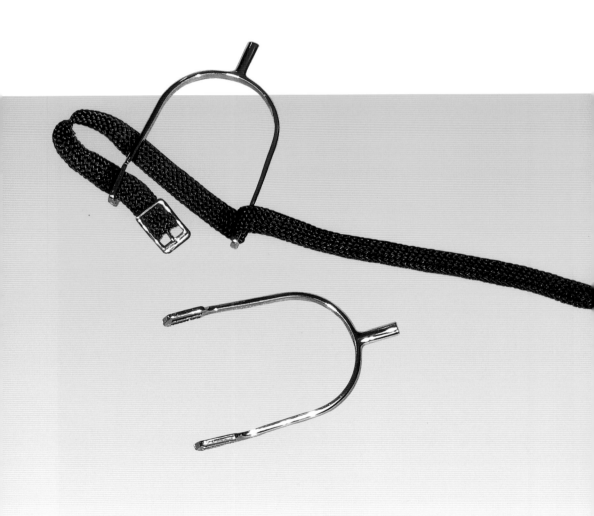

6

Ready to Ride

Ready to Ride

To get the most out of riding, it is essential that you learn to ride properly and take note of all safety precautions. Learning the correct procedures help you gain confidence, understand how to communicate with your horse, read signals your horse is sending you and to deal safely and calmly with any problems that arise. It may seem exciting to simply jump on a horse and gallop away, but this is dangerous, and could lead to injury – both to yourself, and your horse.

What to wear for everyday riding

THIS ILL-EQUIPPED RIDER LACKS A HARD HAT AND PROPER BOOTS. TRAINERS CAN EASILY SLIP THROUGH STIRRUPS.

It is not necessary to spend vast amounts of money on clothes when you first start riding, but there are a few things that you will need. The most important factor in deciding what to wear is safety. Around the yard, wear old clothes for mucking out and tack cleaning. If you are handling ponies – loading them into a trailer, for example, you should at least wear your hat and gloves. You might want to wear a body protector as well, just to be on the safe side.

DO NOT BE TEMPTED TO RIDE IF YOU ARE NOT PROPERLY EQUIPPED – LEAD YOUR HORSE INSTEAD.

Riding hat

Starting with your head, it is essential to have a riding hat. It must be well fitted and at least up

A RIDING HAT IS ESSENTIAL.

to current safety standards. Never buy a second-hand hat, as it may have been dropped or damaged in such a way that it will not provide maximum protection in the event of an accident. If you do drop your hat you should buy a new one. Skullcaps are used most often for cross-country and jumping. You can wear these on their own or with a brightly coloured silk over the top. Velvet-covered hats have a peak and are a smarter choice for shows. Either hat is fine for general riding as long as it is well fitting and has not been dropped or damaged.

Footwear

RIDING BOOTS.

When you first start riding, suitable footwear is of the utmost importance. You should have long rubber riding boots or short jodhpur boots. At the very least, use a shoe with a short heel and smooth sole that will stop your foot slipping through the stirrup. Shoes with a heavy tread such as Wellington boots can get caught up on the stirrup, and are not advisable.

Trousers

For hacking and general riding jodhpurs are the most comfortable and hard wearing. Jeans and other trousers that have a seam down the inside can rub and be uncomfortable. Jodhpurs are available in a wide range of designs and colours. Cream, beige or white jodhpurs are the most common colour for shows and events but, for everyday wear, you can be as bright as you like!

Body protector

This should be of a good safety standard and well fitted. Your saddler should be able to help make sure that you have the correct size.

A BODY PROTECTOR.

READY FOR LOCAL SHOW.

Gloves

Gloves will help protect your hands from blisters or burns from the reins and ropes. They are also essential for keeping your hands warm in the winter. In the summer thinner gloves can be useful, as sweat from a pony's neck can make the reins slippery and the gloves will give you a better grip. Some of them have rubber bobbles to help with this.

Coats and jackets

Aim for well-fitted garments that are not too loose and baggy. Always keep your coat done up when riding in case the flapping frightens a pony. Lighter colours tend to make you more visible to motorists.

What to wear at a show

What you wear to a show will depend on what type of event or class you are entering. For local shows, wear your hat in a hair net if you have long hair, with a shirt and tie and a riding or hacking jacket. Wear white, cream or beige jodhpurs and black or brown riding or jodhpur boots and gloves. Everything should be neat, tidy and clean.

Where to ride

CHECK THAT THE HORSES AT PROSPECTIVE RIDING SCHOOLS APPEAR WELL CARED FOR.

Before you get a pony of your own you need to find somewhere to learn to ride. The most common practice is to find a good local riding school and take a course of riding lessons. A national horse society will have a list of recognised and approved establishments in your area. Visit all the riding schools that you are interested in and make a point of noting whether the ponies look happy and well cared for. Check that the yard looks well maintained, clean, tidy and safe and ask to see if your

instructor is qualified to teach you. Some stables may let you help out before or after your lesson and you will be able to pick up helpful stable management tips. Others have an indoor school and cross-country jumps. Riding holidays at a good establishment are a great way to spend a fun week riding and generally being around ponies. Always make sure that any stables are covered by the appropriate insurance and licence.

Mounting and dismounting

Mounting

It is important that you know how to mount safely. Your pony should stand quietly while you mount and this is one of the lessons a pony will have already learnt. If he tries to walk off when you are mounting, keep a firm hold on the reins and wait for the pony to stand still again. Always check that the tack is correctly fitted before you mount a pony, and make sure that the girth is tight enough that the saddle will not slip as you get on, and that the stirrups are down and about the right length. You usually mount from the near side, which is the left side of the pony. When you are experienced enough, practice mounting and dismounting from both sides.

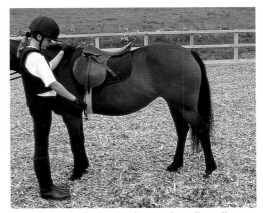

1 Stand by the pony's near-side shoulder and hold both reins in your left hand just in front of the withers. Make sure that the off-side reins are shorter.

2 If you think you might accidentally pull on the pony's mouth as you get on, hold a bunch of mane with the reins.

5 Hold the saddle by the waist on the far side, and spring up. As you swing your leg over, move your right hand from the waist of the saddle to the front, right-hand side of the saddle.

3 Hold the stirrup with your right hand and place your left foot in it.

4 Hop round to face the pony's side and, with your toe pushed downwards so that it does not dig into the pony's side, prepare to spring up.

6 Sit down gently and place your right foot in the stirrup. Take up the reins ready for riding. Check that safety stirrups have the rubber on the outside. If you need to alter the length of the stirrup, do it now. You can do this by holding the reins in one hand and pulling up the end of the opposite stirrup leather to move the buckle to the required hole. You should practice doing this without looking down, although this is not easy to start with. Keep your foot in the stirrup while altering the length. The correct length of the stirrup can be gauged before you mount by placing your knuckles on the stirrup bar. The stirrup iron should reach to your armpit.

Dismounting

1 Make your pony stand quietly before dismounting. To dismount correctly take both of your feet out of the stirrups, put the reins in your left hand just in front of the withers. Place your right hand on the front of the saddle and lean forwards.

2 Swing your right leg over the pony's hind quarters, being careful not to kick it.

3 Land on your toes, bending your knees and avoiding the pony's foreleg.

CHECK THE TACK BEFORE RIDING TO ENSURE IT IS FITTED COMFORTABLY AND SAFELY.

STAND IN FRONT OF YOUR PONY TO CHECK THAT THE STIRRUPS ARE THE SAME LENGTH.

Sitting correctly

CORRECT HAND POSITION.

It is important that you sit in the saddle correctly and that you are well balanced, otherwise it will be uncomfortable for you and the pony and you won't be able to give the aids correctly. Aids are the signals that you use to communicate with the pony. Your bottom should be relaxed in the saddle with your weight in the lowest part, and evenly spread across the seat bones. Try to stay supple and relaxed. The balls of your feet should be in contact with the stirrups, with your heels slightly lower than your toe.

From the side view there should be an imaginary line from your ear, through the shoulder and hip and on down into your heel. Another imaginary line should be seen to go through the pony's mouth, through the reins and your hand and on into your elbow. Your hands should be able to follow the movement of the pony's head, keeping constant and light contact with his mouth, without throwing you off balance.

Holding the reins correctly

The reins flow from the pony's mouth, between your little and ring fingers, then up through your hand and over the top of your first finger. The thumbs are placed on the reins to help stop them slipping through your hands. The elbow, shoulder and wrist must remain supple to allow your hands to follow the movement of the horse's head.

CORRECT LEG POSITION.

HOLDING THE REINS CORRECTLY.

Do not bend your wrists inwards and try to keep your thumbs facing the sky.

Aids

Aids are used to communicate to a pony.

Artificial aids include whips or spurs, and natural aids involve using parts of the body to communicate with the pony, hands, legs and voice, for example. Aids must be given clearly and should be consistent.

Natural aids

Your hands, legs, voice and body are natural aids to communicating with your pony. All aids, whether natural or artificial must be quiet, kind and never hurried, rough or sharp. Your voice, for example, can be soothing for a nervous pony, and he will soon learn simple instructions. Never lose your temper and shout. If your pony is not obeying, it probably means he doesn't understand your command. try again making your instructions clearer.

SITTING SQUARELY HELPS THE PONY TO BALANCE.

THIS RIDER IS LOPSIDED.

Hands

Use your hands through the reins and bit to control speed and direction.

Legs

Use your legs to nudge a pony's side to encourage it to go faster.

Voice

Your voice should never be underestimated as an aid. Talk to your pony constantly, either to calm him down or as praise. In time a pony will learn to recognise the command given by repeated words or phrases such as 'walk on' and 'whoa'.

Your body

The way you sit in the saddle and your weight can be used to send signals to the pony when you are more experienced. Ponies tend to be able to tell from your seat if you are nervous.

IN THE CROSS-COUNTRY SEAT RIDER IS LIGHTER IN THE SADDLE. THE WEIGHT OF THE RIDER IS FORWARD, ALLOWING THE HORSE TO BALANCE EASIER AT FASTER PACES.

Artificial aids

Sometimes a litle extra encouragement is needed to make a pony obey your commands. Use artificial aids sparingly if your horse or pony does not respond to natural aids. Artificial aids can be used to reinforce the messages from natural aids, and in time, your pony may learn to obey the commands from natural aids more quickly.

Whip

A whip should be used to reinforce a leg aid that the pony has ignored. Use it just behind a pony's leg as you repeat the aid with your leg.

When using the whip always take your hand off the reins and place them in the other hand. Never use a whip in anger.

Spurs

Spurs attach to the boots by a strap around the ankle and under the foot. However, they must only be used by an experienced rider who has complete control of their legs at all times.

SPURS

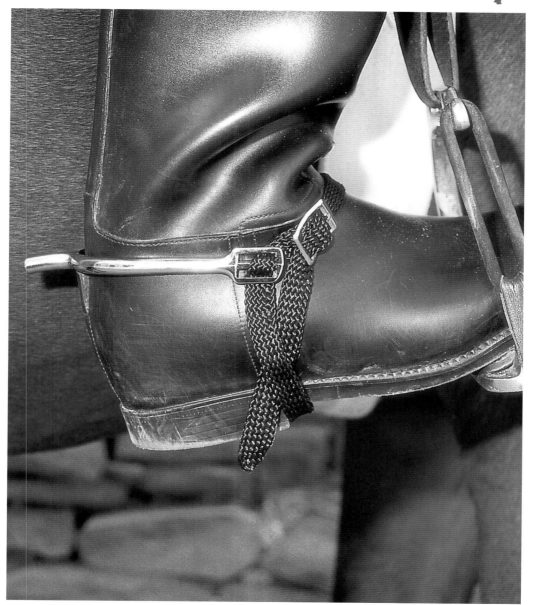

SPURS ARE AN ARTIFICIAL AID USED BY EXPERIENCED RIDERS TO ENHANCE NATURAL LEG AIDS.

Learning to ride

It is important that novices learn to ride properly with a good instructor and in a standard fashion. For the health and safety of both you and your pony, it is simply not safe to launch yourself on to a horse you do not know, particularly if you only have a vague idea of how to control it. Everyone must learn the basics of riding – how to care for a horse, the equipment needed, how to mount and control the animal at different paces, and how to stop. These fundamentals can be learnt in a series of structured lessons and to do anything less is simply irresponsible. Furthermore, without proper instruction, your first riding experiences may well be unpleasant for both pony and rider.

Walking

A pony naturally has four paces. The slowest is the walk, where all four feet are brought to the ground at a different time in a certain order, therefore this pace is called 'four–time'.
This is the order in which the feet come to the ground in walk. The pony has at least two feet on the ground at once.

The aids to ask your pony to walk on from a stand still are to shorten your reins to a length at which you have a light feel on the pony's mouth, and to close your lower legs against his sides. As the pony moves off, make sure that you allow your hands to follow the natural movement of the pony's head. When you are giving the aids to 'walk on', sit up straight in the correct basic position and look forward between the pony's ears. If the pony does not move off willingly, give him a nudge with your lower leg. Even though you are sitting up straight, your body should not be tense.

To halt

Once you are walking you need to know how to stop again! Use the same aids that you use to steady the pace or to slow down from one pace to another. You must close your legs against the pony's sides and take up a stronger contact on the pony's mouth. Release the pressure once the pony has stopped or slowed as you wished. Do not use too much pressure on the mouth and never be rough or impatient, as it is sensitive and easily hurt.

IN WALK, ALL FOUR FEET COME TO THE GROUND AT SEPARATE TIMES, HENCE A 'FOUR-TIME' PACE.

Trotting

The trot is a pace of 'two-time' meaning that the legs are coming to the ground in two diagonal pairs.

The pony springs from one pair of legs to the other as it moves along. There are two ways of 'riding the trot' – sitting or rising. Sitting trot is when you stay sitting in the saddle. Although this is bumpy you should stay in the basic position and allow your body to be relaxed and supple enough to go with the movement of the pony. Always use the sitting trot when changing pace. The rising trot is a way of avoiding the bumping by rising up and down in the saddle with the rhythm of the trot. You sit in the saddle as one pair of feet comes to the ground and rise as the other pair comes to the ground. This takes quite a while to master but is much more comfortable once you get used to it. Make sure that the weight of your body is not in the stirrup, but that you use the inside of your thigh and knee to support you. Keep your back straight and do not tip forward. Do not use the reins to pull yourself up – your hands should not be affected by what the body is doing.

To slow down from trot to walking pace, close your lower legs against the pony's sides and apply a little bit of pressure on its mouth. When the pony has walked for a few steps repeat this method to stop the pony.

DIAGONALS IN TROTTING.

TROTTING.

Cantering

CANTERING IS FASTER THAN TROTTING AND REQUIRES GOOD CONTROL.

saddle and close your lower legs behind the girth. Slowly increase the pressure until the pony strikes off into canter. Do not lean forward as this will encourage the pony to go faster and you will have less control. To decrease the speed of the pony, do as you would when trotting and slow down in stages until you reach a stop. Your first cantering is best done with an instructor in an enclosed area.

Canter is a pace of 'three-time', which means the feet come to the ground as a single foot, then a diagonal pair and then on the last foot. The walk, trot and halt must be mastered and well practised before you attempt to canter, as it is obviously a lot faster and you need to be in control.

After the three beats there is a moment when all four legs are off the ground and are suspended in mid air! When you are more experienced you will be able to feel without looking down which leg is leading when you are cantering.)

To ask your pony to canter, sit well down in the

AT ONE POINT IN MID-CANTER, ALL FOUR LEGS WILL BE OFF THE GROUND.

Galloping

GALLOPING REQUIRES A LIGHTER POSITION IN THE SADDLE, WITH THE WEIGHT FURTHER FORWARD.

Do not attempt to gallop until you are quite a competent rider. To get to gallop from canter is quite easy: you simply close your lower legs and allow the pony more slack on the reins so that he can stretch his neck. Ponies' bodies and strides lengthen when galloping and you must make sure that your hands are free to maintain an even contact with the mouth and be in control at all times. You decrease the pace as with cantering, progressing through all the stages until you come to a halt. Always be sure that the ground you are galloping over is safe without wet, boggy patches or potholes.

Turning

When turning a corner or riding in a circle the pony's body must be bent in the direction you are going with the head looking in that direction.

Aids to turn or circle

Keep your body square in the saddle and face the direction that you intend to go in. Your inside hand (on a circle to the left this would be the left hand) steers the pony where you want to go and your outside hand controls the pace, or the speed, keeping the pony's head in the correct direction. Your legs are used slightly differently too. Your inside leg should stay in its normal position, while the outside leg should be a little behind the girth. Use your inside leg to ask for an increase in pace.

Starting jumping

BEND FORWARD FROM THE WAIST AS THE PONY JUMPS.

Jumping is great fun, but you must be confident in all other paces before starting to jump. Ponies usually enjoy jumping lessons and jumping the odd log when you are out for a hack. If you are just beginning, try not to interfere with the action of the pony when it is jumping. Shorten your stirrups one or two holes to help keep your weight over the pony's centre of gravity.

Trotting poles

There are some things that an instructor may do with you and your pony as an introduction to jumping. Jumping poles laid on the ground are often used to start with. These should be placed about 1 to 1½ m (3 to 5 ft) apart, depending on the size of the pony or horse. The diameter of the poles should be about 10 cm (4 in.). Start by walking over a single pole until the pony gets use to it then move on to a trot. When the pony is happy with this, place two or three poles on the ground about 1 m (3-ft) distance apart and trot over them in a rising trot. These exercises should only be attempted with your instructor. Trotting poles help the rider to develop balance, rhythm and an eye for judging a distance. They have many advantages to the pony as well, helping with balance, rhythm, co-ordination and correct muscle development.

Small jumps

A pony's outline changes as it approaches a jump. It lowers its head and stretches its neck to help balance itself. As the pony leaves the ground, he raises his neck and head and places his hind legs underneath them. The pony jumps upwards, lifting its forelegs off the ground and then the hind legs, and is in mid-air over the jump. His head and neck are stretched out and all four legs are tucked beneath him. When landing, the pony stretches out his forelegs and lifts up his head. The hind legs fall just where the forelegs landed and the pony continues to move off.

Riding position over a jump

1 You must shorten the stirrups by one or two holes to help keep your weight over the pony's centre of gravity. Keep your lower legs in contact with the sides of the pony, giving a squeeze when you want him to take off. As the pony leaves the ground your bottom should stay in contact with the saddle and you should bend forwards from the waist. Grip with the inside of your thighs and knees to keep you in place. Do not stand in the stirrups, keep looking ahead and let your hands follow the pony's head, maintaining contact all the time.

2 As the pony lands and brings up its head, return gracefully back to your normal position. Do not point your toes downwards at any time or it will be much harder to maintain your correct position. Make sure you 'go with' the pony as it jumps. If your lower legs come back too far you will tip forwards putting you off balance. Always jump under instruction to start with to avoid forming bad habits.

Exercises

Exercise will increase your fitness level. You need to achieve a moderate level of fitness to gain the greatest benefits from riding. For those who do not own their own pony, there are some exercises that can be done without using one. Cycling is a good exercise in preparation for riding especially if you stand up to pedal sometimes. It works the same muscles that you use for riding, particularly the thigh and calf muscles. Start slowly and build up gradually. Cycling also helps to make the joints from the hip downwards supple.

Swimming is also an excellent form of exercise. Start slowly and build up the number of lengths you do. Vary the strokes to work as many different muscles as possible. Walking is an essential exercise, with a brisk walk being a very effective way to increase fitness. Start with a short distance, walk energetically and gradually build up distance and pace. Walking can be done almost anywhere and the only expense is a comfortable pair of shoes. Wear loose clothing and walk somewhere safe. Later you can jog for some of the way. Skipping, aerobics and dancing are also all good forms of exercise. Make sure you take advice from a doctor before starting any new exercise.

ALWAYS practice these exercises with a qualified instructor.

Exercise while mounted

You must have a very quiet pony to do these exercises and should always have an experienced person to hold the pony still while

ARMS BEHIND BACK.

BACK BEND.

THE AEROPLANE HELPS YOUR SUPPLENESS.

HOLDING PONY FOR LEG STRETCH.

SUPPLE ANKLE EXERCISE.

you do them. Always ensure that you carry out these exercises correctly as injury may result if you get them wrong. A neck strap (see page 76) will give you something to hold if you start to lose your balance at any point.

Shrug your shoulders up as high as you can towards your ears and relax them; do this a few times.

Stretch your arms above your head and then relax them, bringing them down quietly. Rotate your hands from the wrists in both directions and wriggle your fingers to loosen them up.

Remove your feet from the stirrups and cross the stirrups over in front of the saddle. Then turn your feet in a circular motion in both directions to loosen up the ankles.

Hold the front of the saddle and bring your knees up to the front arch. Move your knees out to the side away from the saddle and lower them back down gently. This stretches the muscles on the insides of your legs.

Raise your arms to shoulder height with your fingers stretched out straight. Bring them into your chest one at a time.

Hold your arms out straight to the sides at shoulder height and turn your torso so that one arm points towards the tail and the other points towards the ears. Keeping your hips square and your legs still, come back to the front and swing smoothly around to repeat on the other side in the same way. This helps to make the waist more supple.

Raise your arms above your head and bend at the elbow, bringing your fingertips down to touch your shoulders then raise them up again.

To strengthen the stomach, fold your arms and lean backwards gently until the backs of your shoulders touch the pony. Then sit up again. Make sure you keep your leg in the correct position. Only do this a couple of times, as this pits quite a strain on your muscles.

Other exercises might be introduced by an instructor, such as riding without stirrups. Riding bare-back and jumping a row of small jumps without stirrups will help improve your balance but they need to be done under the guidance of an instructor, preferably in an enclosed area such as an arena.

Around the world

1 With the stirrups crossed over in front of the saddle, swing your right leg over the withers to sit on the side.

4 Continue around until you are back to your normal riding position.

2 Swing your left leg over the back so you are sitting facing the tail.

3 Swing your right leg over the rump to sit on the right side.

Touching toes

1 Touching your toes is quite hard and if you cannot get all the way do not push yourself. Raise your right arm above your head and stretch forwards and down to touch your left toe.

2 Do the same on the other side. Only do this a couple of times.

221

Riding safely

Riding on the road is dangerous: riders and ponies are killed every year. Here are a few hints to help maintain proper safety on the road and while hacking. Always ride out with a knowledgeable person or instructor until they consider you to be competent enough to be out on your own.

BRIGHT SAFETY CLOTHING IS ESSENTIAL WHEN ON THE ROAD, ESPECIALLY IF THE LIGHT IS POOR.

1. Always listen out for traffic and be aware of the road and its users. Always concentrate on the road and do not stop.
2. You and your pony should wear reflective items of clothing at all times. A large variety of items are available such as fluorescent and reflective hat covers, exercise rugs, tabards for the rider, tail covers, leg and arm bands, whips, jackets, gloves, and boots for your pony.
3. If you are riding out on a hack take a mobile phone, but keep it switched off in case it rings and scares the pony.
4. Wear a watch and keep an eye on the time, particularly in winter when it can get dark very quickly.
5. Always tell someone where you are going and what time you expect to be back.
6. If the road is icy stay near the edge where the horse can get a better grip. Keep your feet out of the stirrups just in case you need to get off the pony quickly. If you come across snow grease the soles of the feet.
7. Take a riding safety course and test in order to learn all of the signals for turning and for asking a vehicle to slow down or pass slowly.
8. Do not canter or gallop on hard or uneven ground.
9. Do not ride on a verge and definitely do not canter on it, as there may be hidden objects, ditches or holes.
10. If your pony goes lame, dismount and lead it home, standing between the pony and the traffic at all times. If you are a long way from home or your pony is very lame then call for help. It is useful to carry a hoof pick with you.
11. Read, learn and always practise the Highway Code.
12. Be polite and considerate to all other road users and always thank someone who is considerate to you.
13. Always wear a well-fitting hat that is up to current safety standards. Keep it done up at all times Riding boots and a body protector are also advisable.
14. Make sure that all your tack and equipment is in good working order before you set out, including any protective boots your pony may need to wear.

RAISING AND LOWERING AN ARM MEANS 'SLOW DOWN PLEASE'.

'I AM TURNING RIGHT'.

'STOP PLEASE'.

Travelling with your pony

Most ponies will travel well in trailers or lorries. However, experience is needed to ensure safety. Protective clothing for the pony and a well-maintained vehicle and trailer or a lorry are essential. Sometimes ponies do not like being locked up in trailers and can resist. Remember that you are asking them to go into a small, confined space which can be frightening, especially if they have had a bad experience in the past.

When travelling never:

- Use a trailer, vehicle or lorry that is not 100% safe and well maintained.
- Drive fast or brake suddenly.
- Travel with two ponies in the trailer without a partition separating them.
- Let anyone travel with the pony in the trailer.
- Get in between the pony and the partition when in the trailer.
- Travel with a pony that is wearing protective boots and equipment.
- Load a pony without wearing at least a riding hat, boots and gloves.
- Load your pony alone.
- Rush loading your pony.

Loading

Try to make the trailer as inviting as possible. Put bedding on the floor and leave the doors at the front open to make it light. A haynet hung in one corner or a bucket of feed will help keep the pony busy. Always have experienced help when loading and unloading, and make sure that you wear your riding hat, boots and gloves and a body protector if you have one. Do not drag your pony into the trailer, but gently walk confidently up the ramp with the pony following. Make sure the pony is not too close to the edge of the ramp as he could fall off it. If he is reluctant to go up the ramp, lift a foreleg and place the foot on the ramp. Then do so with the other foreleg. The pony should then just give in and walk up the ramp. Once the pony is in the trailer he should be fastened in securely. If you are loading two ponies, load the easiest one first as this will often give the second one more confidence to go in. Always remain calm and quiet when loading and unloading because a pony will sense if you are nervous.

ALWAYS LEAD YOUR PONY GENTLY TO THE TRAILER RAMP – DO NOT TRY TO DRAG IT.

LEAD YOUR PONY UP THE MIDDLE OF THE RAMP. IF TOO CLOSE TO THE EDGE, HE COULD SLIP OFF.

THE PONY SHOULD NOW WALK QUIETLY AND CONFIDENTLY INTO THE TRAILER.

Protective clothing

TRAVELLING BOOTS WILL PROTECT THE LEGS.

All-in-one travel boots are the easiest to put on and take off and provide good protection. On the foreleg they reach from the coronet band all the way up to cover the knee, and on the hind legs they go reach from the coronet band up over the point of the hock. If you do not have all-in-one travel boots you can use a stable bandage over padding. A light rug will help keep the pony clean and free from flies. A tail bandage or tail guard is used to prevent the tail being rubbed on the journey. If you use a tail guard you will need a roller to secure it. A poll guard attaches to the head collar behind the ears and will protect the pony should he bump his head. Various other items are available including knee, hock and overreach boots, which are most often used with stable bandages (see page 94). Make sure that you use a sturdy head collar and rope.

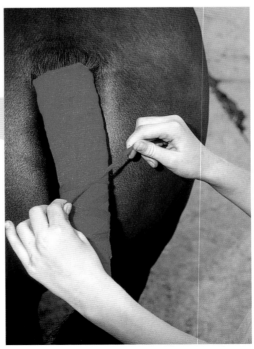

A TAIL BANDAGE WILL STOP THE TAIL BEING RUBBED.

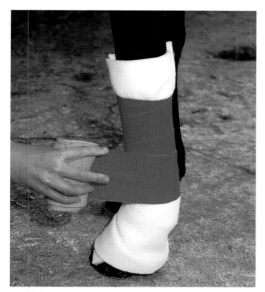

USE BANDAGES IF YOU LACK TRAVEL BOOTS.

Unloading

If you are using a trailer with a front ramp, lower the ramp and untie the pony before undoing the breast bar and leading the pony out quietly. If unloading two ponies, unload the one nearest the front ramp first, then move the partition across to allow an easy exit for the second. If a trailer has just a rear ramp, untie the pony and get a helper to lower the ramp. Stand quietly and encourage the pony to go backwards carefully and slowly, but do not let him try to turn round. Always reward a pony with a pat if it has unloaded or loaded quietly and calmly.

Trailer safety

Always make sure that your trailer or lorry is well maintained and regularly serviced. Pay particular attention to the lights, brakes and hitch, and watch out for the wooden floor, as the boards tend to rot eventually. Make sure all electrics and lights work properly and that you use a safety chain. Check that your ramps are safe and the tyres are the correct pressure.

Riding for the disabled

Ponies are not only therapeutic for disabled people but can have practical uses too. They provide a means of getting around and offer a sense of independence in the way that a guide dog does for a blind person. Mentally or physically disabled people derive a tremendous amount of joy, pleasure and freedom by being able to ride or drive a pony. They often form a deep bond and understanding with a pony. Ponies suitable for the disabled vary, but should always be responsive, well-mannered and kind. Competitions are held for disabled riders and drivers and many are very talented in achieving a high standard despite their disability. Ponies used for driving are often smaller because the cart needs to be low to the ground to allow access for a wheelchair.

7

Horse Sports

Horse Sports

There are many horse sports, and there will be something suitable for almost everyone. Some you can learn yourself with relative ease, while others, like jumping and racing are great spectators sports. You will probably want to try several sports and activities before choosing to concentrate on just one, or you may enjoy them all. You should also bear in mind that not all ponies are suitable for all activities.

Local shows

HORSE SHOWS ARE FUN EVENTS AND ARE SUITABLE FOR ALL LEVELS OF RIDER.

SIMPLE JUMPS MAKE UP THE MOST BASIC JUMPING COMPETITIONS.

Shows start at a local level and go all the way up to international competitions. Local shows, held throughout spring, summer and early autumn, are great fun once you have learnt to ride and are completely in control of your pony. They have a large variety of activities and classes, so there should be something for everyone to enter.

Clear-round jumping is when you pay a small fee to enter a ring full of jumps. If you jump them all in the correct order without knocking any down, and without your pony refusing any you will receive a rosette. Another type of jumping class is where, having jumped a clear round, you go through to the next round or enter a 'jump off', usually set against the clock. Competitors are placed in order with the fastest and clear-round jumpers first. Your age, size and pony's ability will decide which classes you are suitable for.

There are also showing classes such as 'Best Riding Pony' and 'Best Family Pony'. Some judge the appearance and confirmation of the pony, while others concentrate on the ponies' manners and behaviour. 'Handy pony' is an obstacle course where you have to complete

FOR MORE EXPERIENCED RIDERS, SHOWJUMPING IS THE NEXT COMPETITIVE STAGE.

games such as walking over a plastic sheet; hanging washing on a line; posting a letter; dismounting, doing a task, then mounting again; walking past scary things; negotiating obstacles; and walking over and under things. All while managing your pony at the same time!

Gymkhana games are often found at local shows and are great fun as they are a test of how well you can stay in the saddle. Most events involve racing in and out of upright poles. The winner in most gymkana games is the fastest to complete the course. The games are usually run either by the age of the child riding the pony or by the size of the pony. They are good for helping to improve riding. For some show classes you stand a better chance of winning if you plait your pony's hair, while for others it will not make any difference. Fun classes such include 'Veteran Pony', 'Best Pony Kept Out At Grass' and 'Fancy Dress' competitions. All in all it is a great fun day out.

JUMPING EVENTS ARE POPULAR FOR ALL RIDERS.

EVENTS AND SHOWS INCLUDE COMPETITIONS FOR BEST APPEARANCE AND BEHAVIOUR.

Polo

Polo is a popular sport all over the world and has been played for hundreds of years. It was first played in England in about 1800, and is a game where two teams play on a special field with four players in each team. Each player wears a protective helmet and padding and uses a stick with a head made from bamboo A ball made of willow and bamboo is about 7½ cm (3 in.) in diameter and weighs between 100-125 g (4½ and (5 oz). The polo field measures about 274 metres by 183 metres (800 x550 ft). Games last up to an hour and

are divided into sections (or 'chukkas') of 7½ minutes, with 3-minute intervals between them. Half time is about 5 minutes long. Ponies must be agile, fast, responsive and fit. The pony can be of any size. The argentine pony is a popular choice, as it is very agile. Two mounted umpires and a referee oversee the game. To score a goal the ball has to pass between two goal posts. Special training is needed if you want to become a polo player with your pony. Clubs exist in many areas and ponies that are good at gymkana games have been successfully taught how to play polo.

horse sports

Long distance riding

Rides can vary from a local pleasure ride of about 10 miles (18 km) to rides of 100 miles (180 km) spread across one or more days. Any fit pony in good condition should be able to manage fairly long rides, although proper conditioning and preparation is required for both horse and rider. Rides often take you over wonderful countryside and participants are friendly and helpful. You will have to travel to the rides, so transport will be a large part of the cost involved. Most rides have inspections by vets to check that a horse is coping with the work and is still sound.

Any breed of horse can be successfully conditioned to complete long rides, although Arabs are most often chosen for the endurance rides. They seem to be less likely to suffer from leg problems and are strong and courageous.

A pony must have a kind temperament and be reasonably sensible and yet forward-going and willing. Attention to the hooves and shoes is of the utmost importance, as a wide variety of grounds will be encountered on a long ride. Make sure that both you and your pony train and are in prime condition before attempting any long rides.

Eventing

Eventing includes the disciplines of dressage, cross-country and show jumping, and is usually held over one or three days. These events test the all-round ability of a horse and rider, who need to perform well at all three activities to stand a chance of winning.

Dressage involves a written test that has to be followed very accurately and can be done at varying levels of expertise and experience. The horse and rider must perform a particular move at a stated pace in order to gain points. The overall appearance of pony and rider should be smooth and elegant.

Cross-country involves a course of rustic, fairly solid fences over a field or parkland. Obstacles including a water jump and piles of logs for jumping. Usually ridden at a canter or gallop, cross-country tests the strength, skill and stamina of both the pony and the rider.

Show jumping is usually held in an enclosed arena and involves a course of jumps made up of coloured poles and fillers. Faults are gained if a fence is knocked down, if the pony refuses to jump or if you follow the wrong course. If the rider gets a clear round he or she is entered into another round, which is usually shorter but may have higher jumps and is likely to be timed.

You will need to have reached a competent level of riding before you go eventing, and this could give you something positive to aim for. Your instructor will be able to prepare you for your dressage test. Various clothes and items will be needed for each discipline, which could be expensive. The hard hat and boots are the most important safety items for the rider, along with a body protector for jumping. Make sure that your pony is well protected with boots for the jumping section, too. Dressage, show jumping and cross-country events are all also held as separate events, so you may choose to pursue just one discipline.

READY FOR THE OFF!

SHOW JUMPING

SHOW JUMPING

CAPTION

Driving

Driving is very popular and demands a high level of skill, particularly at competition level. Horses and ponies are driven on their own, in pairs or in a teams. Even if you are used to riding a pony, driving is a very different experience. It is important to be competent and confident before attempting to drive alone.

Good breeds of pony for driving include Fell, Dales, Connemaras, Welsh Cobs, Welsh Ponies, Exmoors, Dartmoors and Shetland ponies. Thoroughbreds, Arabs and Hackneys are not so suitable for the novice driver. Other breeds that are seen are Morgans from the United States and Cleveland Bays.

The harness looks daunting to start with and it is important that it is kept in good condition and correctly fitted. It is traditionally made of leather, but these days it can be made of webbing, canvas, felt, buffalo hide and other manmade materials. Once you are competent you can progress to shows, but get your pony used to being driven in company first.

8

Conclusion

Conclusion – A pony of your own

Once you have researched the pros and cons of horse ownership, you will realise that the decision to buy a pony should not be taken lightly. Ponies, like other animals, need a lot of attention. You must provide grazing, fresh water and shelter from the weather in winter and from flies in summer. You must have enough knowledge to care for your pony and/or the help of a knowledgeable friend. You must also be sure that you can afford to buy and look after a pony.

There are many things to consider before you buy your first pony. Age and looks are not as important as good behaviour. The pony should be a suitable size for the child and an experienced older pony is likely to be much more patient and usually less flighty than a young one. A more mature, well-mannered, school master will be much safer and more reliable in the long term. A healthy pony is extremely important. A few sores, blemishes or lumps and bumps are acceptable in a first pony, especially one in its teens or older. However, do get any pony checked by a vet before you buy it, even if you know the previous owner.

THE CHILD ON THE LEFT IS TOO BIG FOR THE PONY, WHILE THE PONY ON THE RIGHT IS TOO BIG FOR THE CHILD.

A GOOD STURDY NATIVE PONY IS IDEAL FOR CHILDREN.

Prices for ponies can vary enormously, and are usually guided by temperament, safety and suitability for children, rather than looks or talent for leaping huge jumps. Take an experienced horse owner with you if you are buying from someone you do not know. A knowledgeable person should be able to tell you if the pony is suitable for your riding ability and where you intend to keep the pony after you have bought it.

Any pony must be good in traffic. Ask to see the owner of the pony riding it on the road when

you come to view it. The pony must be good to shoe and easy to catch. Ponies that are good to travel save a lot of hassle and are much safer.

Be wary of adverts that might bend the truth and take special care when buying from sales and auctions which are sometimes used as a dumping ground for problem ponies. Borrowing or leasing ponies must be accompanied by a legal contract so everyone knows exactly where they stand.

conclusion

EXERCISING IS FUN IN NICE WEATHER, BUT HAS TO BE DONE ALL YEAR ROUND.

All costs must be considered carefully. Take into account routine veterinary care, and the hidden costs of illness, injury and insurance. It is important to be covered for public liability and other things such as loss of tack and death. Find out how much your local farrier charges for new shoes, and remember he will need to visit you every six to eight weeks. Feed costs will vary with the lifestyle, but find out how much hay and hard feed are locally, and the price of the bedding you want to use. Equipment such as grooming, mucking-out equipment, boots

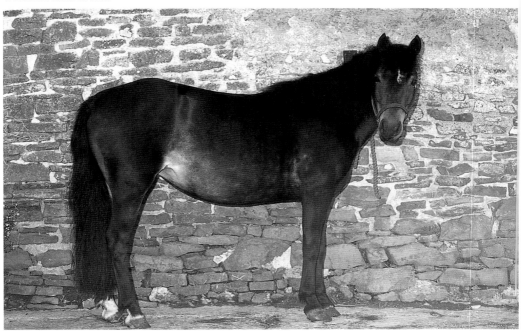

THIS TYPE OF STURDY PONY OFTEN MAKES A SUITABLE FIRST PONY.

and bandages, rugs, numnahs, girths, saddles, bridles, headcollars, ropes, riding clothes and boots, hat equipment and stable equipment need to be taken into account, and the likelihood that they need to be replaced from time to time. If you are going to shows you will need smart clothes, a trailer (and a vehicle to pull the trailer) and entry fees. You will also need livery or rent fees if you do not own your own land and stables. All of these add up, so be very well prepared and ensure that you can sensibly afford it.

DON'T FORGET – THERE ARE LOTS OF CHORES TO BE DONE – IT'S NOT ALL EXCITING!

YOU WILL SOON PROGRESS TO FUN ACTIVITIES LIKE JUMPING.

index

Index

Credits and Acknowledgements

The author and publishers would like to thank the following people for their assistance:

Firstly, Emily, Stephanie, and Sarah Lang, and Daniel Moore for being such excellent models.

Mr and Mrs. Bailey for allowing us to use their facilities in some of the photographs.

The Dorking Saddlery.

Veterinary practice – McFarlane and Associates.

Assistant – Ena Tulloch.

Picture Credits

Pictures pp10, 39, 142 © Stockbye

Pictures pp234, 238,-239, 244 © Photodisk